E.Q. LIBRIUM

E.Q. LIBRIUM

UNLEASH THE POWER OF
YOUR EMOTIONAL INTELLIGENCE:
A PROVEN PATH TO CAREER SUCCESS

YVETTE BETHEL

ORGANIZATIONAL SOUL, LTD.

E.Q. Librium—Unleash the Power of Your Emotional Intelligence:
A Proven Path to Career Success

Graphic Design by: Marcellus Bassett and Stephen Burrows
Cover Design by: Multimedia Mars
Cover Photo: ©iStockphoto/artSILENSE

Organizational Soul, Ltd.
P.O. Box N-511,
Nassau, Bahamas.
www.orgsoul.com

ISBN: 978-0-578-08360-5

Printed in the United States of America
First Edition Printing: November, 2011

CONTENTS

ACKNOWLEDGMENTS 13
PREFACE 15

PART ONE: THE FOUNDATION 19

CHAPTER 1: EMOTIONAL INTELLIGENCE 101 21
    What Is Emotional Intelligence? 21
    The Origin of Emotions 22
    E.Q. Librium Fundamentals 27
    E.Q. Librium and Value Systems 28
    Finding Your E.Q. Librium. 28

CHAPTER 2: E.Q. LIBRIUM AND YOUR PERSONAL LIFE 31
    Emotional Intelligence and Personal Success 31
    Finding Your Purpose 32
    Setting and Achieving Your Personal Goals. 33
    An Integrative Plan. 34
    Knowing When to Quit 34
    Consequential Analysis. 34
    Emotional Intelligence and Communication 36
    Health and Emotional Intelligence 37
    Emotional Intelligence and Stress Management 38
    Personal Financial Management. 38
    Emotional Intelligence and Relationship Building 39

CHAPTER 3: CONNECTING EMOTIONAL INTELLIGENCE
AND YOUR CAREER SUCCESS 41
    Influence 41
    Leadership Strength. 42
    Team Leadership and Participation. 43
    Organizational Awareness 44

Self-confidence 45
Other Leadership Competencies Linked
    to Emotional Intelligence 46

CHAPTER 4: THE LINK BETWEEN EMOTIONAL
    INTELLIGENCE AND ORGANIZATIONAL
    PERFORMANCE 49
Increased Sales Volumes 50
Improved Employee Capability and Morale 51
Enhanced Customer Satisfaction and Brand Strengthening 51
Decreased Turnover 52
Employee Development 53
Balanced Change Leadership 53
Healthy Working Relationships 53
Boundary-Crossing Tactics 54

CHAPTER 5: UNDERSTANDING YOUR EMOTIONS 59
How to Identify Your Emotions 60
Tips for Identifying Your Emotions 61
Recognizing Your Patterns 62

CHAPTER 6: SELF AWARENESS 65
The Glad Game 67
Viral Transmission 67
Sensitivity and Emotion 70
Seek First to Understand 71

CHAPTER 7: MANAGING YOUR EMOTIONS 73
Self Discipline 73
Commitment 74
Resilience 74
Flexible Optimism 75
Tools for Managing Your Emotions 75
The Benefits of Managing Your Emotions 79

CHAPTER 8: LINKING EMOTIONAL INTELLIGENCE
    AND CRITICAL THINKING 81
1. Define the Problem 83
2. Distinguish the Relevant from Irrelevant 86

3. Understand the Reliability of the Source. 87
4. Achieve Objectivity. 87
5. Draw Conclusions and Create Solutions. 87

CHAPTER 9: PURPOSE AND EMOTIONAL INTELLIGENCE . . . 89
Lights On, Lights Off. 89
The Path to Purpose. 91

CHAPTER 10: EMOTIONAL INTELLIGENCE AND
VALUE SYSTEMS. 97
Value Systems 97
Constructive Emotional Intelligence 98

PART TWO: ACHIEVING E.Q. LIBRIUM. 105

CHAPTER 11: GETTING UNSTUCK. 107
Avoid saying "I am too busy". 107
Open the Doors Yourself 108
Set Your Boundaries. 108
Recognize Limiting Patterns 108
Maslow's Hierarchy of Needs 109
Conquer Patterns of Low Self-Esteem 111
Create Tolerance for Risk. 111
Create Your Vision and Mission 112
Put a Stop to It. 113
Shift Your Paradigm 113

CHAPTER 12: ENCOUNTERING EMOTIONS SOCIALLY. 117
1. Jealousy and Envy. 117
2. Blame. 121
3. Voicelessness. 125
4. Self-Protectionism 128
5. Quiet Desperation 130

CHAPTER 13: EMOTIONALLY COMPETENT
COMMUNICATION 133
Maslow's Hierarchy of Needs: A Communication Application. . . . 133
Communication Dynamics 136

The Communication Loop: Encoding 137
The Communication Loop: Decoding 138
Barriers to Listening 138
Nonverbal Communication 139
Tips for Improving Your Communication Skills 139
When Communication Is Not Received As Intended 140

CHAPTER 14: USING EMOTIONAL INTELLIGENCE TO
NAVIGATE CONFLICT 143
Conflict Resolution Modes, Transactional Analysis,
and Emotional Intelligence 143
Integrating the Thomas-Kilmann Model of Conflict
Resolution with Emotional Intelligence 144
Conflict Resolution Styles 145
The Competing Style 146
The Collaborative Style 146
The Compromising Style 147
The Avoiding Style 148
The Accommodating Style 148
Conflict-Driven Environments 149
Navigating Different, Difficult People 150
Types of difficult people 150
Emotionally Intelligent Conflict-Resolution Tools 160
Self-Knowledge 161
Self-Regulation 162
Knowing When to Quit When Faced with Conflict 163
Engaging Others 164

CHAPTER 15: OFFICE POLITICS 167
Overly-Political People 167
Force versus Authentic Power 168
Substance Focused People 170
Politically Savvy People 170
Position Based Power Structures 171
Applying the Thomas-Kilmann Conflict Model to Politics 172
Competing in Political Environments 173
Collaboration Mode 173
Compromise 173

Avoidance 174
Accommodating People 174
The Spectrum of Political Styles 174
Communication and Political Behavior 176

CHAPTER 16: DEVELOPING OTHERS 177
Empower Yourself and Your Team 178
Tips for Developing Others 178
Develop Others through Stretch Projects 179
Coaching Fundamentals 180
Allowing 181
Self-Regulation 182

CHAPTER 17: EMOTIONALLY INTELLIGENT
    LEADERSHIP 183
Leadership Styles 183
Choosing a Leadership Style 186
Emotionally Intelligent Leadership (EIL) Competencies 187
Competence, Commitment, and Engagement 191
Morale Attunement 195
Emotionally Intelligent Leadership (EIL) 196
Emotions and Leadership 199

Chapter 18: EMOTIONAL INTELLIGENCE
    AND DIVERSITY 201
Diversity and Bias 201
Culture and Emotional Intelligence 202
Tolerance vs. Inclusion 203

CHAPTER 19: THE IMPORTANCE OF EMOTIONAL
    INTELLIGENCE TO THE ORGANIZATION
    OF THE FUTURE 207
Hyper-Change Is in the Forecast 207
Transparent Organizations 209
Multigenerational Coexistence 209
New Skills for the Future 210

GLOSSARY 213
BIBLIOGRAPHY 217
WORKS CONSULTED 223
INDEX 225

FIGURES AND TABLES

Figure 1.1: An Emotional Response Process. 24
Figure 6.1: Fundamentals of Self-Awareness 66
Figure 6.2: Sample Emotions and the Responses They Can Evoke 69
Figure 9.1: Finding Your Purpose 90
Figure 11.1: Maslow's Hierarchy of Needs 109
Table 11.1: Reframing Considerations. 114
Figure 13.1: Maslow's Hierarchy of Needs 134
Figure 13.2: Berlo's Model of Communication. .137
Figure 14.1: Emotional Intelligence Applications
        of the Thomas-Kilmann Model of Conflict Resolution 145
Figure 14.2: Model of Critical Feedback 152
Table 15.1: Inauthentic Power Tactics 169
Table 15.2: Authentic Power Tactics 169
Table 15.3: Symbols of Inauthenic Power 171
Figure 15.1: Emotional Intelligence Applications
        of the Thomas-Kilmann Conflict Resolution. 172
Table 15.4: Differences between Political Styles .175

To my mother, late father,
siblings, nephew, and closest friends.

ACKNOWLEDGMENTS

We can only be said to be alive in those moments when our hearts are conscious of our treasures.

—Thornton Wilder

WRITING a book is no easy feat. Many people helped me bring this book from amorphous thought forms into reality. Thanks to Mark Humes for his support in the editing process and to Dr. Lucile Richardson, who helped me to improve the manuscript and bring it to a final version. You showed up at exactly the right time.

Thanks to Marcellus Bassett and his team for the illustrations and tables within this book, and to Max Jones for being a connector. Thanks to Carmen and Justin Kennedy for believing in me through it all. Thanks to Mark Whitehouse, Sharell Ferguson, Lyrone Burrows, Bill Thomson, Tanya Woodside, Philip Simon, Mimi Schroeder, Jared Cyrus, Phil Whitmarsh and his team and Charmaine Bourbon for your honesty and input. A special thanks to Joshua Freedman at 6 Seconds who introduced me to the transformational world of emotional intelligence. Finally, thank you to Martin Sage and all my coaches who helped me along the journey to this point.

To my mother for her unwavering belief in me. Her faith and unconditional support inspires me to remain focused on what makes me come alive: being of service to others. Thank you for always knowing my needs before I do, for accepting my idiosyncrasies, and for always creating an environment of constancy and family.

To my brother, sister, nephew, and late father for enriching my life. To my best friends for supporting me in my quest to be the best me I can be. They believed I had a book within me before I knew or believed.

I also dedicate this book to the many people who allowed me to be of service as a coach and trainer. You brought color, variety, and lessons into my life.

PREFACE

In the last decade or so, science has discovered a tremendous amount about the role emotions play in our lives. Researchers have found that, even more than IQ, your emotional awareness and abilities to handle feelings will determine your success and happiness in all walks of life, including family relationships.

— John Gottman Ph.D.

MANY journeys begin with a desire for personal discovery, development, or actualization. My journey into the domain of emotional intelligence started on what I thought was a simple path: a desire to learn how to manage my emotions. Earlier, I recognized a number of my emotions but had a very hard time managing them effectively, preferring to withdraw whenever my emotions felt assaulted by excessive information. Building my emotional intelligence became a rite of passage when I realized that if I could manage my emotions effectively, I could become more successful and balanced in all aspects of my life.

I also embarked on the journey of building my emotional competence, because the games people play in virtually any situation fascinated me. I started tracking the games people play at work, school, home, and church environments. In the work environment, I observed employees who seemed overwhelmed by the politics when they were forced to engage in overly political work environments. Others basked in the complexity of overly political environments. I also observed people who were emotional time bombs. They erupted with raised voices, demonstrated accelerated speech patterns, created destructive confrontations, and exhibited profound moodiness. These behaviors led to a number of responses that ended up creating entire systems of behavioral patterns. Over time, I started to accumulate a very long list of toxic interactions, and I started to explore how I could put this list to constructive use. One of my responses was to write this book. Another response was to create the simulation, THE GAMES PEOPLE PLAY AT WORK.

In every organization, I witnessed similar emotionally oblivious patterns in leaders and employees and realized most people are blissfully unaware of how their behaviors impact their colleagues. For instance, one person may describe his or her behaviors as passionate, tenacious, and focused. The person on the receiving end may interpret the same actions as argumentative, controlling, bullying, or relentless. Both perceptions are real to the perceivers. If people are not trained to manage themselves and the situations they encounter, the result is often a toxic environment.

Another reason I chose to provide tools to develop your emotional intelligence is that there are tertiary academic systems concentrating predominantly on developing the academic competencies of students. As a result, there are students who are ill-equipped to successfully engage the emotional aspects of workplace interactions. The newcomers enter the workforce with ideals of teamwork, collaboration, and opportunities, but many of them encounter contaminated environments that draw them into a web of negativity and stasis. This book will prepare newly recruited college students to successfully navigate the emotional intricacies of diverse office relationships.

In his book, *Emotional Intelligence,* Daniel Goleman said, "People with well-developed emotional skills are also more likely to be content and effective in their lives, mastering the habits of the mind that foster their own productivity; people who cannot marshal some control over their emotional life fight battles that sabotage their ability for focused work and clear thought." The belief that emotional intelligence leads to self-regulation and that self- regulation can lead to balance is the underlying assumption here. This is exactly what this book is about: creating emotional balance and improving your quality of life.

I was inspired when I found that, unlike our intelligence quotient, our emotional intelligence quotient (E.Q.) can be improved. This means there is hope for anyone who wants to work on building their Emotional Quotient. This was the most compelling reason for writing this book.

E.Q. Librium—Unleash the Power of Your Emotional Intelligence: A Proven Path to Career Success is divided into two parts. In Part One, I examine the fundamentals of emotional intelligence, how it is linked to your success, and the characteristics of emotionally intelligent people. Managing your emotions is an art, so you can choose to use the combination of tools from this book that best fit your personal style and strengths. Part Two provides practical steps and strategies you can use to manage emotionally charged situations. Part Two is also integrative. It presents perspectives of leadership, conflict, politics, and diversity, providing ideas about how to apply emotional intelligence strategies to multiple facets of interactions.

This book is designed to provide you with practical tools that can help you achieve balance through your emotions, no matter your gender, career, family background, plans, or stage in your life.

—Yvette Bethel

PART ONE

THE FOUNDATION

CHAPTER 1

EMOTIONAL INTELLIGENCE 101

It is very important to understand that emotional intelligence is not the opposite of intelligence; it is not the triumph of heart over head—it is the unique intersection of both.

—David Caruso

What Is Emotional Intelligence?

IN 1990, Peter Salovey and John Mayer coined the term *emotional intelligence* and defined it as "a form of social intelligence that involves the ability of monitoring your feelings and emotions and those of other people, discriminating among them, and using this information to guide your thinking and actions."[1]

In creating the term emotional intelligence, Salovey and Mayer clearly distinguished between feelings and emotions. Feelings can happen with or without emotion attached. For example, you can have a feeling that you should do something else with your life, but you may not be clear about what you want to do, how it should be done, or when you should do it. The emotion attached to the feeling may be hope or frustration.

There are a number of philosophies about the difference between feelings and emotions. In the article "The World of Feelings and Emotions," Walter Last made a distinction between feelings and emotions that is similar to my understanding, when he said, "Feelings, in a general sense, are what we may feel in any part of our body. These may be simple body sensations, such as hot or cold, pain, a touch, or else they may be feelings associated with emotions, such as love or hate, joy or anger. Emotions, on the other hand, are feelings or reactions about someone or something, usually involving our ego. We are angry about someone, afraid of something, in love with someone."[2]

> **emotional intelligence:** a form of social intelligence that involves the ability to monitor your feelings and emotions and those of other people, discriminating among them, and using this information to guide your thinking and actions.

One of the first things I learned about emotional intelligence is that it is not about being emotionless. It is really about experiencing your emotions and navigating them so you can interact effectively with the people around you.

There are people who believe that when you become emotionally intelligent, you should be nice all the time. This is a complete misconception. I had a student once who stated that no matter what she did, her emotions made it difficult for her to be nice. I told her that it was more important to express herself appropriately using emotional intelligence than to be nice. I went on to explain that sometimes it is necessary to disagree or be firm, while at other times, it is appropriate to be nice or agreeable. Emotional intelligence provides the skills you need to help you understand that it is okay to disagree and when you do, how to do it constructively.

The Origin of Emotions

When you become emotionally charged, your body experiences a physiological response. Your head and heart interpret the stimulus and apply a label to the situation. Once this happens, you have the choice of making an appropriate or inappropriate response.

> **critical thinking:** exercising or involving careful judgment in evaluating a situation.

CASE STUDY #1: Antoine's Annual Performance Review

Figure 1.1 below articulates the processes by which a person may react to external stimuli. The following case study offers some insight into the process of emotional reaction to external stimuli.

Antoine met with his reporting officer for his annual performance review. Antoine had not met with his reporting officer all year, but he was optimistic because he was sure his performance was above average. Unfortunately, his reporting officer had a completely different perspective about Antoine's performance, articulating disappointment in Antoine's marginal productivity. Antoine was blindsided and crushed by the annual review. He recognized that the points his reporting officer raised were legitimate, but he felt hurt, disappointment, and anger because his supervisor did not tell him earlier so he could self-correct. As a result, Antoine's emotions manifested physiologically as a pain in his chest. He could no longer look forward to the salary increase that would help him to qualify for a new car loan.

Unless you are already adept at reprogramming your responses, your unconscious emotional reactions are usually linked to your experiences. These experiences are linked to your family and religious traditions, personal interests, education, physical appearance, timing, values, current emotional state, vocabulary, body language, and tone of the information exchange.[3] These filters can cause you to make associations, and your response may take only seconds.

While there are differing schools of thought regarding the sequencing of the thoughts and emotions that drive a reaction or response, it is clear that thought and emotion both undergird reactions and responses.

In Figure 1.1, the emotion being experienced is anger, and the person experiencing the anger is also experiencing a physiological response connected to the anger. The action thought that occurs prior to making a response is where there is an opportunity for the person to reframe the experience and respond consciously instead of letting the emotion of anger lead to an unconscious, imprudent response.

An Emotional Response Process

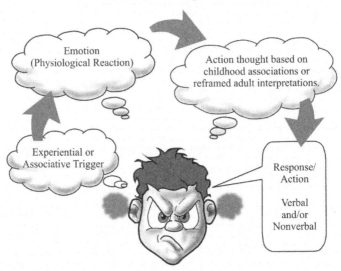

Figure 1.1: An Emotional Response Process.
Source: © 2011, Organizational Soul Ltd.

Emotions are usually categorized as positive or negative, but various researchers assert that emotions are not inherently good or bad but are purely a source of information. We also characterize responses to emotions as good or bad, but again, these responses are a source of information. For example, Jen tells Marsha that it looks like Marsha is gaining lot of weight. Marsha is initially irritated by the comment, but she can choose to respond in different ways that provide Jen with information about the impact of her comment:

Sarcasm: "That's funny; I was thinking the same about you."
Frustrated: "I am tired of people commenting about my weight."
Humor/Self-Deprecation: "Uh oh. No more doughnuts for me at our morning meetings."
Hurt: I thought I was losing weight.

Conceivably, all these responses will invoke a reaction from Jen and provide information about how the statement affected her. When responding while irritated, it is important to consciously decide how you will communicate to ensure your message isn't lost in uncontrolled emotion. If not, the consequences may be irrevocable.

CASE STUDY #2: Michelle's New Job Description

"I want my old position back," Michelle shouted. "You are being unfair to me, and I don't deserve to be treated this way after all these years with the company!"

Until a month ago, Michelle was a proud employee. She recently celebrated thirty years of service with a single employer. She always perceived herself to be a hard-working employee. Her clients know the pride she takes in providing them with quality customer care. Today, Michelle is angry—correction, furious—with her manager because she feels she was unfairly treated.

About a month ago, Michelle's manager, Ed, called her into his office to inform her that she was being placed in a new position at a lower level because of a recent restructuring exercise. Michelle was shocked and became disoriented. The change meant she would have a new supervisor and a job description similar to the one she had earlier in her career.

Michelle was now adamant that Ed did not give her a fair opportunity to learn the new skills necessary for her to be successful in a new job at her previous higher level. Ed's perspective was different. He felt he made an extra effort to assign an employee from another department to provide Michelle with a second round of personalized, one-on-one training before the position changes were announced.

So, Ed was confused and annoyed by Michelle's accusation. Michelle agreed that she was supposed to receive additional training but felt the employee wasn't able to provide the individualized instruction, because the trainer was given additional duties to perform while she was supposed to be training Michelle.

Michelle's new supervisor, Tanya, was frustrated, because she wasn't sure how to resolve this situation. Which side should she take? On one hand, the manager produced concrete evidence of his attempt to train Michelle. On the other hand, Michelle's arguments make sense, and she does exhibit valuable customer service strengths. Tanya has to find a way to resolve this situation and maintain the team's respect.

Tanya was confused, frustrated, and cautious, because she was in the middle of a stalemate between her reporting officer and a member of her team. She knew she had to manage this situation with skill. On one hand, she had an employee completely demoralized by the restructuring and who was affecting other employees. On the other hand, she had a manager who produced concrete evidence that the employee was given special treatment that no one else was afforded. As a result, Tanya decided to put her emotions aside and review the facts. Because of her approach, the appropriate course of action eventually became clear.

From Tanya's perspective, Michelle was now in a position with less responsibility. Although the customers still sing her praises, Michelle is not meeting Tanya's performance expectations. While Michelle's performance may have been influenced by factors such as her emotional state, a lack of adequate training, or level of competence, Tanya cannot consider supporting Michelle's reinstatement at the higher level unless it is justified by performance levels. After reflecting on the situation, Tanya realized she was not in a position to support Michelle's request for reinstatement, but she could provide Michelle with coaching and developmental opportunities.

When Tanya communicated her views about the situation, Michelle was understandably disappointed but realized the conclusion was based on an objective consideration of the facts and not emotion or bias. By basing her decision on contextual realities, Tanya was not obligated to determine who was telling the truth; she circumvented the need to take sides, because she knew this would generate an emotional response and cause division. Consequently, Michelle respects Tanya as her reporting officer, and Ed respects Tanya as a leader.

I am sure there are a number of ways this situation could have been resolved effectively, but Tanya used her emotional intelligence, critical thinking, and strategic skills to maintain balance within the team. The primary message of this case study is that emotional intelligence is not the only driver of success, but it is an inextricable part of the equation for success.

E.Q. Librium Fundamentals

The term *E.Q. Librium* specifically refers to your ability to use your Emotional Quotient (E.Q.) to achieve balance or self regulation in emotionally-charged situations. E.Q. Librium is achieved when you are able to identify both your emotions and the emotion of others and you can filter that information into a balanced, holistic, and self-regulated response. When you build your capacity to balance your emotions internally, you can become a positive influence within a group. The more people in a group who can navigate their emotions, the more effective the group will be at collectively finding a sense of balance, particularly when there are diverse personalities at play. Achieving E.Q. Librium means attaining conscious personal and team emotional attunement.

There is no guarantee that members of the team will choose to manage their emotions as they work toward accomplishing team E.Q. Librium. In reality, freedom of choice is an inherent characteristic of social systems, so it takes conscious effort to influence others to follow the path toward E.Q. Librium. It also takes emotional competence to know when your efforts are not working.

> **E.Q. Librium:** the ability to identify personal emotions and the emotions of others and filter that information into a balanced, holistic, and self-regulated response.

Seeking E.Q. Librium in a team environment does not mean you will always find a solution that will make everyone happy. In fact, your decision may be profoundly unpopular. What it does mean is that leaders are equipped with the skills to listen with empathy, manage morale through realistic optimism, and address the fears of the team. Additionally, leaders can facilitate multichannel flows of information so relevant information is continuously moving to and from the right people at the right times, and issues are being addressed.

E.Q. Librium involves using emotional intelligence to bring emotional balance to a situation and presupposes there will be a variety of emotions experienced both individually and among members of a group. The process for achieving E.Q. Librium involves integrity, fairness, curiosity, objectivity, and accountability, despite prevailing emotions.

E.Q. Librium and Value Systems

I learned early on in my research that just because people possess strong emotional intelligence competencies I could not presume that they have a value system that includes traits of integrity, fairness, or forgiveness. Strong emotional attunement and navigation skills can be used to consciously wreak havoc or to bring balance. E.Q. Librium asserts that team building, integrity, fairness, compassion, and open communication systems characterize the value system driving your emotional balancing activity.

> **value systems**: a set of consistent personal and cultural values used to determine ethical integrity.

Finding Your E.Q. Librium

Your personality is a unique patchwork of strengths and weaknesses woven together in a distinctive pattern that makes you who you are. Your emotions are an important part of this patchwork because we are physiologically wired to experience emotion.

Emotionally intelligent employees are better equipped to find E.Q. Librium and navigate change initiatives by managing themselves effectively. Whether they resist planned changes initially, these employees are able to adapt and contribute to a healthy change environment. They are able to adapt because they understand the consequences of their actions. They are able to navigate their emotions and can put themselves into the shoes of the decision makers. They are effective communicators who possess skills that allow them to navigate office politics that surface when change initiatives are announced.

E.Q. Librium is a powerful tool that can be used to bring emotional balance and stability to volatile situations. According to David Lennick, executive vice president of American Express Financial Advisers, "Emotional competence is the single most important personal quality that each of us must develop and access to experience a breakthrough. Only through managing our emotions can we access our intellect and our technical competence. An emotionally competent person performs better under pressure."

Lennick identifies emotional competence as the primary skill necessary to create transformation. In volatile situations, emotional competence can help you to break a stalemate and move the conflict into a phase of de-escalation and restoration.

E.Q. Librium will help you to seek solutions that will serve the greater good, and because this approach may not be palatable to everyone affected by your decisions, it can help you to manage the fallout. In reality, maintaining E.Q. Librium is an art, and you may have to try several different strategies before finding one that brings the stability you seek.

---

1 Peter Salovey and J. D. Mayer, "Emotional Intelligence," *Imagination, Cognition, and Personality, 9,* (1990): 185–211.

2 "The World of Feelings and Emotions," by Walter Last, accessed December 2009, http://users. mrbean.net.au/~wlast/Feelings.html

3 David K. Berlo's message-centered model of communication (*The Process of Communication* [New York: Holt, Rinehart, and Winston, 1960]).

CHAPTER 2

E.Q. LIBRIUM AND YOUR PERSONAL LIFE

In the last decade or so, science has discovered a tremendous amount about the role emotions play in our lives. Researchers have found that even more than IQ, your emotional awareness and abilities to handle feelings will determine your success and happiness in all walks of life, including family relationships.

—John Gottman

EMOTIONAL intelligence is a derivative of the more mature science: social intelligence. Social intelligence, as described by the psychologist, E. L. Thorndike, is the ability "to understand and manage men, women, boys, and girls—to act wisely in human relations."[1]

Emotional intelligence is a tool that can help you understand and manage your emotions so that you can interact more effectively with the people around you.

The body of emotional intelligence knowledge evolved into a separate science in 1990. Since then, researchers have conducted studies that point toward the linkages between emotional intelligence, personal development, career success, and corporate profitability.

Emotional Intelligence and Personal Success

Personal success definitions differ depending on individual value systems. Here is a sample list of ways emotional intelligence is integrated into personal and professional success strategies:

1. Finding your purpose
2. Setting and achieving your goals despite what people think about your ideas
3. Creating a plan that integrates all aspects of your life
4. Developing the skill of knowing when to quit
5. Understanding the consequences of your decisions
6. Using emotional intelligence to improve communication
7. Managing your emotions to maintain an effective personal health regimen
8. Managing your emotions so you can manage your stress
9. Integrating emotional intelligence into your financial management practices
10. Using emotional intelligence to maintain healthy relationships

Finding Your Purpose

When I was in the process of deciding what I love to do, my life coach suggested that I design a project that would help me to find a career that stimulated my curiosity. My first project was a themed coaching party with friends. The party had a beauty theme and invitees were given one simple instruction. They were asked to wear something they would never wear because it makes them feel uncomfortable. One person arrived in a ball gown, another arrived in a bikini, and yet another participant came in a mini dress. We talked about beauty and coached one another, challenging each other's beliefs about beauty and pointing out imperfections that were attractive, so the process was transformational for everyone. After that first event, I was hooked on transformational work.

life coach: a professional individual who guides people to their greatest potential, overcoming obstacles, and making commitments that demonstrate measured progress. A life coach works one-on-one with a client to support personal growth, behavior modification, and goal-setting.

For many people, tapping into their depths to discover their purpose is not an easy proposition. Where do you start? Either you do many things well, or you just don't know what you are passionate about, because you haven't explored yourself enough to determine what fulfills you at a deep level. You may have limited exposure, insufficient support, or not enough personal motivation. If you can't tap into your purpose on your own, a coach can help you to move out of a state of ambiguity.

Setting and Achieving Your Personal Goals

In my daily interactions, I meet a number of employees who expect their employers to notice their outstanding work. Most of these employees do not have their own career action plans, so they patiently wait for their reporting manager to call and say, "Congratulations! We recognized your talent and decided to promote you."

One commonly used manipulation that can lead to a state of perpetual waiting is the statement, "We have plans for you." While your employer may have plans for you, it may not be a concrete plan. Even if it is, the role or timing of the new placement may not align with what you want. This can lead to endless frustration, so it is important to engage your intrinsic motivation and create your own plan.

Some employees decide to continue to wait for a promotion after being told there are plans for them, because the vague promise feeds their needs for acknowledgment and promotion. Other employees buy into this statement because they have a strong sense of entitlement. They wait, sometimes for more than a decade, expecting the acknowledgment to become a reality regardless of their competence. This sometimes works whether or not the employee is the best person for the job. Some entitled employees remain with the organization so long that they are eventually promoted by default, because they are the best choice at the time. Some employees define this as success because they are more focused on the result than the deficient process that got them there.

> **action plan:** a focused, disciplined, and thoughtful approach to achieving goals. This includes career and personal goals.

Don't get me wrong. The waiting game is sometimes justified, but there is the risk of disappointment because of the law of numbers. More specifically, there are usually more people waiting and hoping for a promotion than there are vacant positions.

An Integrative Plan

Ideally, your personal goals should extend beyond your career, so creating a career action plan should focus your attention on various aspects of your life and future. For example, if you have a job that requires endless overtime, and you are a newlywed, starting a family under your current work arrangement might be difficult. If you are required to work overtime and don't want this lifestyle, an action plan that you've designed can help you to achieve your personal success goals.

Knowing When to Quit

Many people are taught to persevere. This can be sage advice in the right context, but let's consider the other end of the spectrum. Knowing when to quit is an infrequently contemplated skill. Knowing when to quit can mean you decide to research your options, find a new job, let go of your point, forgive someone, or move out of a relationship and move on with your life. The energy behind knowing when to quit is not the same as giving up. It means you recognize when you have hit a wall and know it is time to recalibrate without losing sight of the end goal.

In any situation, if you recognize you have passed the point of diminishing return, a decision to walk away or change direction may be appropriate. I am in no way advocating running away from your challenges, because they will inevitably follow you. What I do support is summoning the internal fortitude to say, "No more!" and to stand behind your decision despite the dissonance your decision may cause among the people around you. What is most important is to tap into your intrinsic motivation and do what is best for you at the time.

Consequential Analysis

Finding your purpose and setting goals are only part of your journey toward E.Q. Librium. Emotional intelligence improves the quality of the journey to purpose, because skills such as consequential analysis help you to effectively navigate your emotions. Consequential analysis involves considering the consequences of alternative actions before determining your next step. Let us take a look at a series of questions about a career change designed to help you explore what you want to do, how you want to do it, and the possible consequences of your actions:

1. Should I leave my employer?
2. If so, when is the right time to leave?
3. Do I have what it takes to run my own business or should I find another job?
4. If I stay, what do I aspire to and how should I work toward achieving my goals?
5. Do I need to develop new skills? What are they?
6. Will I be able to support myself financially?
7. How would a decision to make a change in my career impact my life plans?
8. Who are the primary stakeholders in my decision?
9. How would my decision affect them?
10. Am I motivated enough to do what I want, no matter what?
11. What are the pros and cons of each option?
12. If damage control is necessary, what is my plan?

> **consequential analysis:** the ability to identify and understand the consequences or alternative results of one's actions.

Whenever you make a decision, it is important to ask yourself a series of questions designed to help you to explore the various facets of the challenge. Circumventing your emotions and exploring different aspects of the challenge can help you understand the consequences of your actions and make carefully considered decisions which will help you to avoid being blindsided by an unexpected outcome.

Emotional Intelligence and Communication

Applying emotional intelligence does not presuppose communication will be easy or seamless, but it does provide you with an arsenal of tools you can use to navigate emotions in difficult conversations. Emotional intelligence is also helpful if the person with whom you are attempting to communicate is unresponsive. Depending on the situation, a lack of response may be clear in meaning or it may further obscure the circumstances. No matter the difficulty in communication, applying emotional intelligence helps you to put your emotions in perspective so you can focus on an appropriate response, keeping the consequences in mind.

Listening is an underutilized communication skill that is often talked about and not always effectively applied. We all struggle with internal thought trajectories that take us away from a conversation. The different types of listening range from combative to passive to active. Typically, active listening involves paraphrasing what you heard and probing to get a better understanding of the message being communicated. Using emotional intelligence to maintain balanced listening and constructive communication means you are attuned to your emotions and capable of navigating their potency.

> **active listening:** an engaged listening mode that allows the listener to understand and evaluate what is being said. The skills of paraphrasing information from another party and using probing questions to gain a better understanding are typically used to clarify the meaning of what is being said.

Listening can happen at multiple levels. If you are able to achieve deeper levels of listening, where you are adept at deciphering nonverbal information, you can detect subtle or implied messages. However, the reason behind the subtle information is not always clear, so you can use your emotional intelligence to mine for more concrete information, if it is available.

Health and Emotional Intelligence

In a 1991 study included in *Learned Optimism: How to Change Your Mind and Your Life*, Dr. Martin Seligman, chairman of the Positive Psychology Center at the University of Pennsylvania, was able to demonstrate the correlation between optimism and better physical and mental health.[2] Seligman asserted that as an optimist, you are empowered and able to do something about your circumstances; you just don't sit around all day in an immobilized victim state.

Pessimists have a different point of view. Seligman asserted that "the defining characteristic of pessimists is that they tend to believe that bad events will last a long time, will undermine everything they do, and are their own fault. The optimists, who are confronted with the same hard knocks of this world, think about misfortune in the opposite way. They tend to believe that defeat is just a temporary setback or a challenge, and that its causes are just confined to this one case."[3]

CASE STUDY #3: Chuck's Physical Appearance

Chuck was always proud of his health and physical fitness. Until recently, he had a toned physique and even offered health advice to co-workers. Within the past year, he was too busy to exercise, worked long hours, and adopted unhealthy eating habits. Because of his new lifestyle, Chuck gained forty extra pounds and was embarrassed by his appearance. He felt unattractive and self-conscious because people who knew him well were shocked by his weight gain. Right now, Chuck is feeling powerless, defeated, and frustrated, because he cannot make the time to exercise and eat right. Emotional intelligence competencies—particularly optimism, navigating his emotions, and consequential thinking—can help Chuck break out of his immobilized state.

In an optimistic state, you have a more balanced view of your state of health, feel personally empowered, can perceive ways to help yourself, and can remain motivated even when your health, diet, or exercise regimen doesn't go exactly as you anticipated. In an optimistic state, you can adapt to new, complicating input without being overwhelmed, destabilized, or permanently demotivated.

Emotional Intelligence and Stress Management

Stress happens if there is a change in your personal or career circumstance that triggers an emotional response within you. It occurs when you are overwhelmed by the change.

Navigating your emotions so you can adapt to controllable and uncontrollable changes that affect you is an important stress-busting strategy. A stress test authored by Dr. Tim Lowenstein[4] lists a number of events in life that create high stress levels. Some of the items on the list include uncontrollable factors, such as the death of a spouse, injury, or illness, trouble with a reporting officer, or a change in a family member's health. Interestingly enough, many of the items on the list can be the result of a personal decision, such as marriage, a new mortgage, a change in schools, retirement, or divorce. Instead of wallowing in an emotion that perpetuates a stressed-out state, it is more useful to develop emotional competencies that can help you to evolve.

Personal Financial Management

For people with limited income, budgeting, delayed gratification, managing debt, and living within ones means are characteristics undergirded by emotional intelligence. For instance, sometimes the pressure to keep up with your peers is hard to ignore. We sometimes view the possession of material items as badges of honor or achievement, and this creates the pressure to acquire those things. Emotional intelligence will set off warning signals if you step outside the boundaries of your budget. On the other end of the continuum, people with significant spending power who are unable to enjoy their wealth because of their fears, can develop their emotional intelligence competencies to help them learn to spend a little more on themselves and give to others.

If you manage your finances from a place of emotional competence, you are focused on your goals and not influenced by material acquisitions of your peers. You may think about the consequences of your purchases, considering whether they will deplete your savings or whether you can pay your bills next month. You weigh the pros and cons of delaying a purchase. You operate from an optimistic state, realizing you may not be able to afford a purchase today, but you know that it is within your power to plan for the purchase. Your mantra: *There has to be a (legal) way!*

Emotional Intelligence and Relationship Building

Emotional intelligence is useful to determine the relationships you should build, redefine, and pursue. It helps you to understand the consequences of your actions and the necessity for relationships.

CASE STUDY #4: Kathy's Mistrust of Co-workers

Early on in her career, Kathy trusted her co-workers to share the workload and operate from a place of integrity. She was an extrovert with ideals about teamwork and collaboration. Over time, she realized her assumptions were incorrect. The people she worked with only cared about themselves and did not always perform their duties with integrity, so Kathy decided to disconnect and complete her tasks with minimal team interaction.

Over time, Kathy's relationships disappeared because she withdrew into herself. Then she started noticing less-qualified people being promoted, and she felt unfairly overlooked. Kathy didn't realize that her emotions of betrayal and hurt caused her to withdraw from relationship building in the work environment. This decision crippled her reputation within the company, and by extension, her capacity for upward mobility.

---

1 E.L. Thorndike, "Intelligence and its Uses," *Harper's Magazine*, 140, 1920, 227–235.
2 Martin Seligman, *Learned Optimism: How to Change Your Mind and Your Life.* (New York; Knopf, 1991).
3 *Ibid.*
4 "Life Stress Test," by Dr. Tim Lowenstein, 1997, accessed January 2010, www.stressmarket.com.

CHAPTER 3

CONNECTING EMOTIONAL INTELLIGENCE AND YOUR CAREER SUCCESS

EI-based abilities more often than IQ-type abilities or technical skills are the discriminating competencies that predict who among a group of very smart people will lead most ably. This is a key point for anyone running an organization who must decide what abilities to look for in potential leaders.
—Daniel Goleman

IN 1997, L. M. Spencer Jr. conducted a study among 300 executives from fifteen global companies.[1] The results revealed that the most successful executives possess emotional intelligence competencies that impact their skills of influence, team leadership, organizational awareness, self-confidence, leadership, and achievement drive. Although the study was conducted among executives, all employees can benefit by developing these skills at various levels.

Influence

As an employee or manager, you participate in meetings where you may not be the one with authority or formal power, but you still have a desire to contribute to the quality of the conversation, decision making, execution strategies, and results. Influence starts with knowing what to say, when to say it, what to ask, and how to say what needs to be said so that you can have a voice. It may mean lobbying before or after the meeting, regulating your emotions, or getting the facts by researching statistics.

I have witnessed instances where emotions crept into a discussion, and the emotions completely derailed the conversation, rendering the person attempting to contribute or influence powerless and voiceless. I have also witnessed situations where emotion was skillfully invoked to override objective evidence, a tactic people use to create an emotional connection when they have limited factual support.

> **influence:** the power to affect, control, or manipulate something or someone; the ability to change the development of fluctuating things such as conduct, thoughts or decisions; an action exerted by a person or thing with power over another.

Leadership Strength

In "Emotional Intelligence and Leadership Effectiveness," by Robert Kerr, John Garvin, Norma Heaton, and Emily Boyle, the authors stated, "It has been claimed that, astonishingly, almost 90 percent of success in leadership positions is attributable to emotional intelligence (EI)."[2]

Employees may not always buy in to their leaders' messages, but, based on observation, they are more likely to respect and trust the emotionally intelligent leader who is fair-minded and displays integrity. Employees in this type of environment are more inclined to remain open to the direction taken, trusting their manager or executive to do what is in the best interest of the team.

Emotionally intelligent leaders are fair and focused on keeping themselves and others accountable, making the hard decisions no matter what the relationship is with the employee. For instance, there are situations where the wrong decision is made to promote an employee. Ideally, if the right position becomes available, a new decision should be made, but emotions, such as guilt, pride, embarrassment, or fear of the consequences of corrective action, can create inertia.

It takes courage to make tough decisions and follow through. Fear immobilizes some managers, so they just complain about the situation and avoid taking any action that could be construed as unpopular. They sometimes perceive the consequences of their actions but lack the intrinsic motivation to make the decision, because they want to be liked or accepted. In cases like these, leaders prefer to sacrifice trust in order to be accepted. On the surface, this reasoning seems counterintuitive, but I am not convinced that they contemplate how their inaction can lead to the erosion of trust, because their primary value is external acceptance.

Emotionally intelligent leaders recognize the different strengths in their team members, peers, and reporting managers and apply leadership basics, changing their leadership style based on the circumstances. For instance, a company hires a consultant for a project. The consultant brings obvious value to the team, but she sometimes arrives late for important meetings. The manager perceives this tardiness as disrespectful, but she doesn't let her emotions override the reality that the consultant is one of the best in the field and brings obvious value to the table. In this case, the manager weighed the outcome of applying pressure for the consultant to be on time versus the significant value the consultant brings to the table and opted not to pursue the issue aggressively.

Team Leadership and Participation

Author Peter Jordan of Griffith University stated, "Research reveals that emotional intelligence is an important factor in predicting performance in teams."[3] Jordan conducted a study entitled, "Emotional Intelligence in Teams: Development and Initial Validation of the Short Version of the Workgroup Emotional Intelligence Profile (WEIP-S)." This study revealed four distinct emotional constructs within the context of teams. They are:

- awareness of your own emotions;
- management of your own emotions;
- awareness of others' emotions; and
- management of others' emotions.[4]

Team leadership and participation are influenced by the emotional intelligence of each team member. Once members of the team are aware of their own emotions and are able to exercise self-discipline, they are in a better position to become aware of and navigate the emotions of others. When emotional intelligence is part of everyday conduct, team members listen actively and express their ideas respectfully and without fear. Team leaders also realize that they can't think of everything, so they are open to input, change, and challenges.

They oppose bias that diminishes the voice of others or creates status because of favor.

> **awareness:** the state of possessing or having realization; a demonstration of perception of a person or concept.

Emotional intelligence skills can contribute to your political skill, helping you develop the right relationships in a way that is beneficial to you—or better yet, is mutually beneficial. It can also help you consider multiple contributing factors and assimilate the information into a viable response while simultaneously managing your emotions. For example, you may be in an environment where your input is requested but not valued unless you say what management wants to hear. Instead of regurgitating the desired response, you can find a way to communicate your point without seeming dogmatic or even worse, without being branded as someone who is not a team player. This can be done through building relationships based on trust. Those relationships allow you to express a different opinion without the threat of a negative label.

Organizational Awareness

Edgar Schein, a prominent theorist of organizational culture defines culture as "a pattern of shared basic assumptions that the group learned as it solved its problems of external adaptation and internal integration, that has worked well enough to be considered valid and therefore, to be taught to new members as the correct way to perceive, think, and feel in relation to those problems."[5]

Executives and business owners are typically the primary architects of organizational culture. They consciously or unconsciously determine which behaviors are rewarded or who is recognized. They demonstrate values, norms, symbols, and rules of the game that are emulated.

For instance, it is interesting to observe employees within a corporate culture that values monetary incentives. It is most notable that once the financial incentives are available, effort is evidenced as around-the-clock, tireless exertion, coming in on weekends and consistently going the extra mile. Once the cycle changes and the incentives are discontinued, the same driven employees change their effort level. In a case such as this, it appears that motivation occurs primarily through the application of incentives and not through relationships.

> **organizational culture:** a codified system of behaviors and mannerisms that is taught to a group and transferred to new members. It is the set of beliefs, values, and norms, together with symbols such as events and personalities that represent the unique character of an organization, and provide the context for action in it and by it.

Emotionally competent employees understand the dynamics of organizational culture and how it affects them. They recognize when they are the right fit for the organization, and they know they have the power to make decisions about their careers. These employees know their value systems and whether their personal values are aligned with the values of the company. Emotionally competent employees are internally motivated to do what is best no matter what anyone thinks about their decision and are willing to make mistakes and adjustments when appropriate. Emotionally intelligent employees don't see themselves as victims of their circumstances; they perceive their circumstances as transitory or temporary.

Self-confidence

I once encountered an executive who had the ability to create the ideas, confidence, and drive to bring a plan into reality. If the plan was trending into the zone of ineffectiveness, he knew when to back off and recalibrate before it was too late, applying creativity to find another way to achieve the same result. He believed firmly in his ideas and was able to focus on how to make them happen, regardless of the curve balls that came his way. The people around him were inspired by his confidence and respected and trusted him because of his values.

> **self-confidence:** self-assuredness in and self-awareness of one's personal judgment, ability, and power.

Confidence exudes from deep within, and it is the midpoint between arrogance and reticence. It emanates from faith in yourself and a true understanding of your strengths and weaknesses. It also comes through the development of emotional competencies of self-regulation, optimism, intrinsic motivation, and purposefulness.

Other Leadership Competencies Linked to Emotional Intelligence

In the article, "Exploring the Link between Emotional Intelligence and Cross-Cultural Leadership Effectiveness,"[6] in the *Journal of International Business and Cultural Studies*, Anne Reilly and Tony Karounos of Loyola University cited additional leadership competencies linked to Emotional Intelligence:

Social Skills: As a leader, your emotional intelligence is inextricably connected to your social skills. In fact, the science of emotional intelligence is a derivative of social intelligence.

Transformational/Charismatic: Competencies such as empathy, optimism, navigating your emotions, and consequential thinking help leaders connect with their teams and build a safe space where trust can be built. Creating a trusting space can drive transformation if the trust is nurtured.

Motivation: Drive undergirds motivation because it helps you to stay on course no matter how your reality appears. You remain focused, optimistic, and empowered. You are able to keep your team focused and productive. Emotional competencies, such as intrinsic motivation, optimism, empathy, and navigating emotions can help you remain driven and motivate others.

Team Awareness: Emotional intelligence is about maintaining and understanding your personal emotional balance as well as providing the skills you need to identify and respond to the emotional states of the people you are leading.

Directed: Patanjali once stated, "When you are inspired by some great purpose, some extraordinary project, all your thoughts break their bonds; your mind transcends limitations; your consciousness expands in every direction; and you find yourself in a great new and wonderful world. Dormant forces, faculties, and talents become alive, and you discover yourself to be a greater person by far than you ever dreamed yourself to be."[7] As a leader, your purposefulness is the force behind your actions that keeps you focused, directed, and result-oriented. Helping others realize their purpose can also help the team.

Participative and Supportive: Emotionally intelligent leaders interested in achieving E.Q. Librium comprehend the importance of teamwork and collaboration. They understand that participation and support lead to synergies, creativity, innovation, and reciprocity, so they demonstrate and reward these behaviors.

1 L. M. Spencer, L. M., Jr., *Competency Assessment Methods: History and State of the Art.* (Boston; Hay/McBer, 1997).

2 Robert Kerr, John Garvin, Norma Heaton, and Emily Boyle, "Emotional Intelligence and Leadership Effectiveness," in *Leadership & Organization Development Journal*, Vol 27 # 4. Pp. 265–79

3 Peter J. Jordan, "Emotional Intelligence in Teams: Development and Initial Validation of the Short Version of the Workgroup Emotional Intelligence Profile (WEIP-S)," in *Journal of Management & Organization*, 2004.

4 *Ibid.*

5 Schein, Edgar. (2001). "Organizational Culture and Leadership." *Classics of Organization Theory.* Jay Shafritz and J. Steven Ott, eds. 2001. (Fort Worth: Harcourt College Publishers).

6 Anne Reilly and Tony Karounos, "Exploring the Link Between Emotional Intelligence and Cross-Cultural Leadership Effectiveness," in *Journal of International Business and Cultural Studies.*

7 Satchidananda, Sri S., *The Yoga Sutras of Patanjali: Commentary on the Raja Yoga Sutras.* (Buckingham, Virginia; Integral Yoga Publications, 1990).

CHAPTER 4

THE LINK BETWEEN EMOTIONAL INTELLIGENCE AND ORGANIZATIONAL PERFORMANCE

Yes! Emotional intelligence can increase organization productivity by increasing leadership performance.

— Reuven Bar-on, Ph.D.

I N the Medrad case study, author Bill Benjamin tells the story about a manager who was receiving exceptional performance reviews but was told if his behaviors did not change, the company would have to terminate him. The manager had to enroll in an emotional intelligence seminar, and upon enrollment he said, "I thought I would sit through the program to appease management and get my attendance checked off. Quite frankly, I saw emotional intelligence as a waste of time."[1]

In a follow-up coaching session, he stated, "I now realize that I was operating with only half of what I needed to be successful— similar to rowing a boat with only one oar." According to Bill Benjamin, "The emotional intelligence training and coaching that the manager participated in made him more aware of his impact on others and identified some gaps he needed to address." The manager eventually admitted, "The training really opened my eyes to things like the importance of learning to react more skillfully when I'm frustrated."[2]

While this case is about a manager, the same is true for business owners, executives, and employees. Organizations with the foresight to invest in building emotional intelligence at the individual level can drive enhanced interpersonal relations, strengthened leadership, higher-performing teams, and improved results. The benefits of developing emotional competencies at the individual level can translate into the following outcomes:

1. Increased sales volumes
2. Improved employee capability and morale
3. Enhanced customer satisfaction
4. Brand strengthening
5. Decreased turnover
6. Employee development
7. Balanced change leadership
8. Healthy working relationships

Increased Sales Volumes

In a 2003 study, "Developing Effective Salespeople: Exploring the Link between Emotional Intelligence and Sales Performance" authors Dawn R. Deeter-Schmelz and Jane Z. Sojka asserted that "training in emotional intelligence (EI) offers a means for developing the communication and interpersonal skills needed by salespeople to develop and improve relationships with customers."[3]

Salespeople who demonstrate the emotional intelligence skills of influence, achievement drive, self-management, self-confidence, and leadership are able to engage clients no matter their level of sophistication. Emotional intelligence is an especially useful tool when a customer is irate. When clients are frustrated, an emotionally intelligent salesperson can focus on the facts and not be drawn into an angry, emotional exchange.

Emotional intelligence is also useful when salespeople need to remain optimistic in the face of low sales volumes, deals that fall through, indecisive clients, or tough negotiations. While some sales are transactional, there are others that require building relationships, and relationships generally introduce the need to manage emotions both intrinsically and extrinsically. The more adept salespeople are at managing emotions, the more effective they can be at selling.

Improved Employee Capability and Morale

In a 2009 article entitled "Assessing Trust," Joshua Freedman stated, "When your people trust you, they dig deeper, listen better, and forgive more readily. When trust is low, there is more resistance, more fear, and communication doesn't work as well (because people don't believe each other, focus on [covering your assets], and defend)."[4] If you don't trust employees to do their work, you may overload yourself or team members with an unproductive employee's work. This usually makes people feel they are overwhelmed. Another example is when you don't share important information with the appropriate people, because they may misuse, misinterpret, or inappropriately leak information.

There are untrusting employees who continuously focus on what is going wrong, who should be the object of blame, or how management is always up to something sinister. These thoughts are not motivating and are driven by pessimism. From an emotional intelligence perspective, optimism is needed to induce improved morale.

> **morale:** a state of individual psychological well-being based upon a sense of confidence, usefulness, and purpose; the mental and emotional disposition of a group with regard to tasks and functions of group operation.

In his book, *Learned Optimism*, Martin Seligman asserted that optimists are more motivated than pessimists. Optimists maintain higher levels of achievement that can translate into productivity, and they have significantly better health. Seligman believed optimism can be learned by reframing negative belief systems that become automatic internal recordings. Therefore, if leaders can learn and demonstrate optimism with the objective of infusing optimism into their teams, one result could be to improve morale by helping the team to view challenges and change from a constructive perspective.

Enhanced Customer Satisfaction and Brand Strengthening

Word of mouth is a powerful branding tool. Satisfied and dissatisfied customers verbalize their experiences. Therefore, it is important for managers and business owners to build the emotional intelligence competencies of their employees so they can master the art of saving the brand. Building emotionally competent employees will help build the heart of your organization and contribute to a strengthened brand that can withstand the assault of difficult times.

While it is clear that numerous factors contribute to strengthening or weakening a brand, employees are an important factor. When managers and employees approach one another with respect and heart, employees can connect with one another and clients, creating the deep connections that sustain business. Mutually respectful, authentic, self-regulated communication leads to a concentration on issues, and if emotions need to be explored, they can be discussed without igniting emotional overflow.

Decreased Turnover

I have facilitated countless exit interviews over the years, and it is evident that leadership is one of the primary reasons employees leave a company. This anecdotal evidence is supported by an article in *Workforce* entitled "Knowing How to Keep your Best and Brightest," which reported the results of interviews with 20,000 workers who were departing from the Saratoga Institute in Santa Clara California.

The primary reason employees chose to leave their jobs was poor supervisory behavior. The article went on to say that "a recent Gallup Organization study based on queries of some 2 million workers at 700 companies found the same results. It's not so much opportunities for raises or promotion through the ranks that keep employees happy. The length of an employee's stay is determined largely by his relationship with a manager."[5]

I agree that employees are more motivated to stay with a company if they have a voice and feel valued. In various exit and career development interviews I conducted over the years, employees shared that they can always use more money, but the ones who enjoy their work environments have managers who value and develop their employees. Leaders who can connect authentically with their employees using leadership and emotional competencies can reduce turnover because of leadership deficiencies. It is important to note that managers who are supportive are not perfect, and they are sometimes as frustrated as their support staff, but trust, value, heart, and voice are all intact.

Employee Development

The emotionally intelligent leader will develop members of the team. They are unafraid of better, smarter, more efficient, or younger team players. They view the potential of team members as an opportunity for their own growth and development. They refrain from control tactics. Instead, they freely coach and mentor support staff because they realize the more creativity they are able to unleash, the better the team performs and by extension, the better the team leader performs.

Emotionally intelligent leaders find a way to balance the cost of employee development versus the cost of underdeveloped employees. They see the benefit of creating targeted learning strategies designed to develop the people in their areas of strength, so they can strengthen synergies within the team.

Balanced Change Leadership

Implementing change in any environment is a balancing act. Change leaders have to balance content, process, and the needs of the people involved in the change to move skillfully through the chaotic stage of change and stabilize at a higher level of productivity.

In most changing environments, there are early adopters, people who sit on the fence and take a wait-and-see approach, and the well-known resistors. Effective change leaders use emotional intelligence skills of pattern recognition, optimism, self-management, consequential thinking, empathy, and purposefulness to pay attention to the dynamic needs of the team in the midst of change. They read nonverbal messages, listen actively, engage conflict in a constructive way, and help members of the team navigate their fears of the unknown.

Healthy Working Relationships

In a 2005 article by the National Association of Church Personnel Administrators entitled *The Individual and the Institution: Strengthening Working Relationships in the Church*[6] the author enumerates the characteristics of healthy working relationships as quality communication, setting boundaries, a willingness to apologize, an ability to see other perspectives, and the willingness to show appreciation. Based on experience, I suggest a few additions to the list: the ability to demonstrate curiosity, sound judgment, and integrity.

Authentic communication undergirds any healthy relationship. As already established, the ability to maintain respectful communication is contingent on your ability to manage your emotions and your reactions to your emotions.

Setting boundaries is another important characteristic of building healthy relationships. When boundaries are consistently encroached upon in a relationship, unnecessary friction can occur if these boundaries are not managed firmly, consciously, and consistently. For some people, you only have to set the boundary once; for others, you have to manage your boundaries every time you meet, because of their predisposition to crossing boundaries.

In the workplace, different executives place varying degrees of importance on trust, but there is no escaping the reality that when trust is impaired, productivity is impacted. In *Five Dysfunctions of a Team*, author Patrick Lencioni asserted that "in the context of building a team, trust is the confidence among team members that their peers' intentions are good and that there is no reason to be protective or careful around the group. In essence, teammates must get comfortable being vulnerable around each other."[7]

Trust and integrity are linked, so integrity is an important characteristic of healthy relationships. If conversations are characterized by integrity and respect, space can be created for vulnerability. Keep in mind the fact that vulnerability will not surface in some cases when there is honest communication. For instance, some people prefer not to take the softer approach to communicating with honesty, so they are blunt and perceived as judgmental with their feedback. While there is integrity with the content, the underlying judgment destroys the integrity of the exchange. In cases such as this, the intention is to give truthful feedback, but the consequence of the delivery can immobilize the receiver of the message, because no one wants to be humiliated. If the hurtful, truthful comments are constant, they can be construed as abuse or harassment, so self-regulation is necessary to ensure you are being constructive.

Boundary-Crossing Tactics

Boundaries can be crossed through verbal communication, but they can also be crossed through other types of actions. Sometimes a person may not recognize a boundary was crossed right away, because there are times when boundary crossing is subtle. Other times it is quite obvious.

Communication is a commonly used conduit for boundary crossing. It can come through body language or volume and pace of speech. It is most obvious when the content of the communication exchange is insulting, aggressive, condescending, or dismissive.

One example of a boundary that is often crossed is when a person refuses to acknowledge a mistake and does not apologize. When this happens, it is demoralizing for the people who are offended by both the behavior that deserves an apology and by the lack of empathy. If you are unable to admit error, you will not be trusted, because this inability is perceived as a reflection of a deficiency in integrity.

When jobs are not clearly defined, boundary crossing can happen. In such situations, each person can develop a sense of his territory being encroached upon. One way this can manifest itself is that one person may perceive another as trying to show him up, and this can happen through severe criticism or unhealthy competition to get an aspect of an overlapping job done.

When change initiatives occur, comfort zones are sometimes destroyed between employees and their supervisors, because everyone has to adapt to the change from point zero. For instance, if withholding information was an important source of power, the announcement of a change can destabilize the repositories of the soon to be out-of-date knowledge, because their source of power is rapidly losing relevance.

Some boundary crossers are convinced that their worldview is the only perspective. This type of thinking is not emotionally competent, because it devalues other insights that can lead to an improved solution or deeper insights. The conviction that there is only one way, combined with the steps they take to ensure there is only one view, serve to erode relationships and cause stagnation and low morale.

Gossip is another type of violation of boundaries, as it is focused on the exposure of information perceived as private or confidential by the target of the gossip. The unfortunate thing about gossip is that it is usually spiked with exaggeration, innuendo, and drama to extend the life of the topic. This type of boundary infraction can be very difficult to recover from as trust erosion is unavoidable and sometimes permanent.

There are people who do not recognize or appreciate others, because they don't want to cause the person being recognized to become puffed up or "full of herself." Others don't recognize the people around them because they don't think anyone is ever good, smart, or effective enough. There are also managers or employees who don't acknowledge other people's achievements because they are afraid the competent newcomer with potential is being lined up for a job at the next level. The employees in each of these cases are high performers delivering superior results. Unfortunately, given the dynamics of the situation, a boundary is being crossed. Two consequences of a lack of recognition or appreciation are a high cost to any organization: employee turnover and low morale. Emotional intelligence skills of empathy, optimism, and consequential thinking can help leaders to take a more balanced approach to reward and recognition.

> **gossip:** idle talk or rumor, especially about the personal or private affairs of others. It forms one of the oldest and most common means of sharing (unproven) facts and views, but also has a reputation for the introduction of errors and other variations into the information transmitted.

Boundary crossing can be positive and developmental. Positive boundary crossing can happen when a manager decides to develop an employee by taking him beyond his zone of comfort because the manager detects latent abilities or talents.

Emotion is usually an indicator that a boundary is being crossed. Fear, anxiety, frustration, or anger are examples of emotions that can arise and create tension both internally and externally. If you are emotionally self-aware, you can identify your emotions and related patterns, then course correct after weighing the possible solutions and consciously selecting an optimal response.

When boundaries are compromised, so is trust. Therefore, the act of establishing boundaries involves personal power or confidence building and mutual trust construction.

Overall, developing your emotional intelligence competencies as they relate to boundary crossing can lead to building healthy relationships, better performance, and an enhanced quality of work environment. Whether you are a manager or employee, you can save time, generate synergies, improve creativity, manage difficult people and situations, and increase your earning power individually and collectively.

---

1 "Emotional Intelligence Training: Case Study—Medrad," by Bill Benjamin on the Selfgrowth

website, accessed December 2009, http://www.selfgrowth.com/articles/Emotional_ Intelligence_Training_Case_Study_-_Medrad.html.

2 *Ibid.*

3 Deeter-Schmelz, Dawn R. and Jane Z. Sojka, "Developing Effective Salespeople: Exploring the Link between Emotional Intelligence and Sales Performance," in *International Journal of Organizational Analysis*, (Vol 11, Iss:3 (1993) pp. 211–20.

4 "Assessing Trust," blog entry by Joshua Freedman at the Six Seconds website, accessed October 2009, http://www.6seconds.org/blog/2009/01/assessing-trust/.

5 "Knowing How to Keep Your Best and Brightest," 2001 article in *Workforce by* Kevin Dobbs, accessed February 2010, www.workforce.com.

6 National Association of Church Personnel Administrators, *"The Individual and the Institution: Strengthening Working Relationships in the Church"* Vol 1, Issue 30, (2005).

7 Patrick Lencioni, *Five Dysfunctions of a Team*, (Hoboken, New Jersey; Jossey-Bass; 1 edition 2002) p. 195.

CHAPTER 5

UNDERSTANDING YOUR EMOTIONS

We have to become more conscious of our feeling-world. By learning to iden-
tify the 'emotional baggage' and manage our feeling- world reactions, we
can view life based on current information instead of being held captive by
our past.

—Doc Childre

CASE STUDY #5: Vera's New Project

Vera told Marie she was excited and appreciative about the opportunity, because one of her career goals was to take on more responsibility. While the project was exactly what she wanted, it required longer hours, and Vera was unable to spend extra time at work. Vera was pleased that Marie was rewarding her with a developmental opportunity, but she was distraught, because she was going to have to turn down the offer—and turning down an offer today may disqualify her from being considered in the future.

Vera was an administrative assistant and a strong performer. In her last annual appraisal, her reporting officer, Marie, described her as very productive with the potential to take on additional responsibility. As a result, Marie, decided to test Vera's potential by giving Vera a project she knew would challenge her both technically and behaviorally.

When Vera received the stretch assignment, she felt mixed emotions. Her first reaction to the news of the project was butterflies, which she attributed to not knowing whether she would be successful with the assignment. In reality, Vera was experiencing an intense mixture of emotions. Marie observed Vera's body language and was curious about what was going on with her, so she asked Vera how she felt about the assignment.

Vera's excitement and appreciation was mixed with helplessness, disappointment, and anger. Each emotion was tied to a thought. Vera was thinking, "Wow, I finally have an opportunity to grow and learn and show them what I can do." This thought was overshadowed by a second thought: "But I have to say no, because there is no pay increase, and I can't afford to pay a babysitter after-hours every day. This is not fair!" Vera was not fully aware of the entire range of her emotions, so she allowed the disappointment to overcome her and adopted a pessimistic outlook. As a result, Vera didn't even consider alternatives that could help her accept the opportunity, and she told Marie that she was unable to accept the opportunity for personal reasons.

This example demonstrates a fundamental reason why it is important to be able to identify your emotions. In this case, Vera allowed herself to sink into a disempowered mode in a situation where a little optimism, brainstorming, and skilled negotiation may have helped her accept the opportunity.

How to Identify Your Emotions

THE first step in identifying your emotions is to expand your personal vocabulary of emotions so you can perceive your full range of emotions and distinguish subtle differences. With a personal emotional vocabulary, your emotions can evolve from being a chaotic ball of vague reactions to a connected ball of definable and manageable emotions. The larger your vocabulary of emotional descriptors, the better equipped you will be to navigate your emotions.

You can build your list of emotions over time. Whenever you experience an extraordinary circumstance, you can add to your list of emotions so that you can accurately perceive your patterns of reaction.

Tips for Identifying Your Emotions

Basic emotions can occur either singularly or in clusters. It is important to note that no matter how many emotions occur at once, if you are not emotionally competent, you will not be able to identify or separate any of them.

Sensations within your body can signify emotions, but sensations may not give you specific information that can help you to separate your emotions.

Alternatively, your emotions can generate behavioral responses that can give you hints about what you are experiencing. For instance, when an abrasive colleague communicates with you, you may experience a general feeling of stress. In response you may develop a behavioral pattern of avoidance that can indicate fear, but your response may also signify anger that you are suppressing.

Another tip for identifying your emotions is to monitor your thoughts. Are you thinking about retaliation or support? Are your thoughts optimistic or pessimistic? You can begin to identify general types of emotions by improving your emotional vocabulary. An expanded emotional vocabulary can help you to make distinctions between emotions you are experiencing. For instance, there are differences between happiness and excitement; anger and rage; or indifference and being unconcerned.

> **self-discipline:** correction or regulation of oneself for the purpose of personal improvement. Having the ability to control one's desires and impulses.

Once you are able to identify your emotions, your ability to build constructive dialogue while in an emotional state will take time, practice, and self-discipline. It is important to note that an appropriate response can show up as anger, sadness, or disappointment, because emotional intelligence is not about being nice all the time; it is about being appropriate.

Recognizing Your Patterns

Your ability to recognize patterns is directly related to your capacity to make the connection between your reaction and the thought associated with it. If you can connect your reactions to the associations driving your responses, you can reprogram yourself to react to situations that would usually trigger an unconscious response.

Building your ability to recognize patterns within yourself strengthens your capacity to recognize patterns in the people around you, and if you can recognize the patterns of others, you can reduce the probability of being blindsided by the unexpected.

CASE STUDY #6: Ralph's Mood Swings

Ralph was in the same job for twenty-five years. He always received top performance ratings, because he was highly productive and loved his work. Ralph usually got along with his co-workers, but from time to time, he was moody and abrupt. His mood swings were predictable, and although his co-workers seemed to like him when he was in a good mood, they tended to avoid him, because they didn't want to get entangled in conflict. Ralph's reporting officer considered promoting him early on in his career, but decided against it because of his concerns about Ralph's moodiness and perceived inability to effectively lead a team. Ralph could not understand how his mood swings were hurting his career. The more his co-workers received promotions, the more frequently he had mood swings.

Ralph can start to improve his career prospects by building his capacities to recognize his emotions and the related patterns of behavior. These skills will give him the information he needs to understand his emotions and navigate them in a way that can turn his career around.

As you become proficient at identifying the behavioral patterns of the people in your immediate circle, understand that you may not be consistently accurate about diagnosing the emotion behind their patterns, so avoid making assumptions. You can gather the facts by asking the person about their reaction, if this is appropriate, because you may not need to know why a reaction happened. Most times, you will not be given insights by the person reacting, because the reason may be unconscious or private.

Think about your friends, family, and co-workers who openly display their emotional states; they are easy to read, and their actions are predictable. Wearing your feelings on your sleeve can make you a target for mischief because predictability can put you in a disadvantaged position. Therefore it would help you to learn to regulate the amount of information you provide through your verbal and nonverbal responses.

CHAPTER 6

SELF AWARENESS

According to [Daniel] Goleman, perhaps the most important emotional competence is that of self-awareness, knowing one's internal states, preferences, resources and intuitions. Self-awareness, the key to increased personal and organizational performance.

—Johann Diaz

S ELF-AWARENESS is a fundamental building block for improved emotional intelligence. Emotions are inevitable, so your ability to identify the emotion or combinations of emotions you are experiencing is critical in developing your ability to recognize patterns of behavior.

Figure 6.1 illustrates the assertion that self-awareness drives both your personal and interpersonal pattern recognition skills. The better you are at identifying your emotions, the more skilled you will be at identifying the emotions and correspondent patterns of others. If you are unaware of your emotional patterns, and you are surrounded by people who are emotionally self- and socially aware, you can be manipulated by them, because they are able to predict your reactions. If others can predict your reactions, and you cannot predict your own patterns, you can be blindsided by unexpected reactions.

Our emotions are linked to our physiology. In the article, "Mind and Body: The Physiology of Our Emotions" by Vreni Gurd, she stated, "When we think of the mind, we think of the flow of information and emotion in a non-material sense, but mind can also be viewed as the communication network between the material body and the brain. Therefore, we can acknowledge that mind and body are actually one and that there is an intelligence associated with the system—it is not simply mechanical hardware, reflexes, and electricity as was once believed."[1]

Fundamentals of Self-Awareness

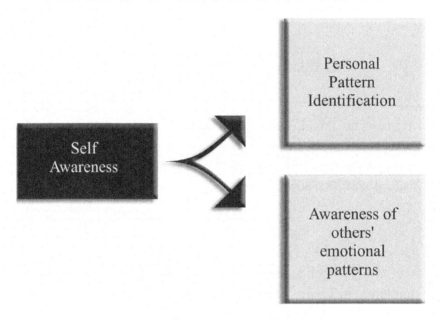

Figure 6.1: Fundamentals of Self-Awareness
Source: © 2011, Organizational Soul, Ltd.

Mind or consciousness leads to manifestation in the body. According to Dr. Candace Pert, emotions link the major systems of the body into "one unit that we can call the body mind."[2] In her words, "We can no longer think of the emotions as having less validity than physical, material substance but instead must see them as cellular signals that are involved in the process of translating information into physical reality, literally transforming mind into matter. Emotions are at the nexus between matter and mind, going back and forth between the two and influencing both."[3] An example of this is when you are nervous and feel butterflies in your stomach or when you talk about a gut reaction.

Recognizing your physical responses can help you understand your emotions and related patterns of behavior. You can use your physical responses to explore what is going on with your emotions, so you can identify what is occupying your mind. For example, Selma woke up in the middle of the night with hives on her arms and legs. Whenever this happens, she takes a step back and explores what is going on with her, because sometimes her anxiety level related to work is so constant that she is not recognizing the stressors are slowly compounding.

The Glad Game

There are some people who refuse to acknowledge that they reacted in a less than supportive way. They have a Pollyanna approach to their circumstances that obscures their view of themselves. Pollyanna is a fictional character who was an orphan who went to live with her wealthy Aunt. Pollyanna always played The Glad Game, which was a game where the players tried to find something to be glad about in any situation. In reality, The Glad Game can be effective if it is undergirded by optimism and integrity. If not, The Glad Game can be a game of self-deception built on fallacy that leads to negative outcomes.

For instance, if someone is insincere about their support, most people will see through their pretense, and this will most likely lead to distrust and the deterioration of morale.

Viral Transmission

In the article, *Managing Emotions in the Workplace: Do Positive and Negative Emotions Drive Performance?* Professors Sigal Barsade, and Donald Gibson asserted that "The process of emotional contagion is a primary mechanism through which emotions are shared and become social, creating collective emotion."[4] Excitement and elation are transferred from one person to another just as easily as sadness, anger, or hope. So another reason for developing the ability to identify your emotions is that once you can identify your emotions, you can seek to determine if the feeling you are experiencing is a result of your emotion or if you were infected by someone else's emotional virus.

> **emotional virus:** the transference of emotion and emotional responses from one party to another.

CASE STUDY #7: Wendal's Misinterpretation of Good News

Wendal was very excited about his recent promotion and shared the good news with his close friend, Mandy, who works for a different employer but feels her talents are being constantly overlooked. Despite Mandy's lack of a promotion, Wendal thought she would be excited about his promotion. Unfortunately, when Wendal told Mandy his good news, his excitement forced her to look at the reality of her undesirable career circumstances. In reality, Mandy was disappointed with her career stagnation and angry with her employer for not recognizing her consistent contributions. As a result of this thought process, Mandy responded to the news of Wendal's promotion with an obligatory and sarcastic response: "Congratulations. I am happy for *you.*" Her body language and intonation reflected her anger and disappointment, and she abruptly changed the subject.

Wendal thought Mandy would be happy for him, but when she wasn't, her less-than-enthusiastic response caught on like a virus because Wendal believed that Mandy was exhibiting jealous behavior. This assumption changed Wendal's emotional state, and he regretted telling Mandy about his good fortune. In fact, instead of an excited virus being transmitted to Mandy, it was transmuted; her anger virus was transmitted to Wendal, changing his excitement to disappointment and anger because Mandy's response appeared to be aloof and jealous. This unconscious model of emotional transmission through communication, occurs when old associations and thoughtless announcements trigger automatic emotional reactions, which can lead to misunderstandings and impaired relationships.

An emotional virus transferred from one person to another can mutate depending on the receiver's filters. This can happen whether or not it is not the sender's intention to project a negative virus. Not understanding emotional patterns and the consequences of your actions can lead to an unwanted or unexpected transmission.

As stated earlier, emotions are not inherently positive or negative; they provide information. Observers assign the labels of positive or negative to emotions, because of their filters based on the perceived thoughts behind the emotions. In fact, witnesses may have differing perceptions of the same situation that range from positive to neutral, to negative. However, for the purpose of understanding how emotions are transmitted, let's classify them into three categories: Positive, neutral, and negative.

Sample Emotions and the Responses They Can Evoke

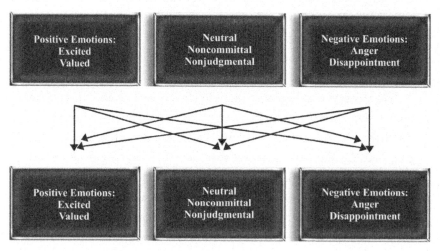

Figure 6.2: Sample Emotions and the Responses They Can Evoke.
Source: © 2011, Organizational Soul Ltd.

Figure 6.2 illustrates how emotions are either transmitted or transmuted as they move from one person to another. Specifically, positive messages can evoke positive, neutral, or negative responses depending on the filters of the receiver of the message. The same is true for all other types of messages.

An emotion can mutate into any other type of emotion either immediately or over time. Here is an example of how emotions can transmute over time because of unconscious behavior.

CASE STUDY #8: Helen's Upcoming Wedding

Helen is very excited about her upcoming wedding to Tony. It is all she talks about at home and work. At first, most of her co-workers were happy for her, and only a few were jealous.

After hearing about the wedding repeatedly over two months, many of Helen's co-workers who were initially happy for her, started to become weary, because they were tired of hearing the same thing repeatedly. Helen misread their boredom as jealousy and became uncomfortable. Her discomfort morphed into anger, so she didn't invite her co-workers to her wedding. Not inviting her co-workers reinforced the rift that was created by her unconscious behavior.

What happened here was that Helen was excited and most of her co-workers shared her excitement at first, so the happy virus caught on. Then Helen's excited wedding chatter continued day in and day out, because she was unaware that her wedding details were not exciting to her co-workers anymore. She perceived their lack of enthusiasm as jealousy and generated the angry virus, which spread because the people with whom she shared most of the wedding details were not invited to attend. All Helen had to do was to notice that her wedding chatter was causing a change in receptiveness.

Sensitivity and Emotion

When you are functioning in an emotional state, you will encounter people with varying degrees of sensitivity. According to Elaine Aron, author of *The Highly Sensitive Person,* "People differ considerably in how much their nervous system is aroused in the same situation, under the same stimulation."[5] Aron also said, "Highly sensitive people [HSPs] do take in a lot—all the subtleties others miss. But what seems ordinary to others, like loud music or crowds, can be highly stimulating and thus stressful for HSPs."[6] In other words, HSPs experience the world and emotions in Technicolor.

Being in an emotional state when communicating with an HSP can translate into withdrawal from the conversation or even an unexpected confrontation.

So, when communicating from an emotionally intelligent place, it is important to recognize how the person with whom you are speaking is wired. It is effective to adapt your communication style so that the listener can accurately receive your message. If you don't know the person very well, there are sometimes clues in his nonverbal behavior that can help you manage the exchange of information.

Seek First to Understand

In *Seven Habits of Highly Effective People* by Steven Covey, the fifth habit is a very important tool in building emotional competence. It is to "seek first to understand, then to be understood."[7] Self-awareness is especially useful in helping you understand others. How can you perceive past the surface of any situation if you don't understand the root causes of your own behavior? To understand the other person, you will need to listen empathically, putting yourself in her shoes so that you can understand her before you seek to be understood.

Self-awareness is the portal to awareness of others. It is also the basic building block for developing your capacity to create strategic, conscious responses to emotionally-charged situations.

---

1 "Mind and Body: The Physiology of Our Emotions," blog by Vreni Gurd, accessed September 2009, http://trusted.md/blog/vreni_gurd/ 2007/03/17/ mind_and_body_psyche_and_soma#axzz1IVx4HTbF.

2 Candice Pert, *Molecules of Emotion*, (New York; Simon & Schuster; 1 edition, 1999)

3 *Ibid.*

4 Sigal Barsade and Donald Gibson, "Managing Emotions in the Workplace: Do Positive and Negative Emotions Drive Performance?" *Academy of Management Perspectives* (February 2007) p. 42.

5 Elaine Aron, *The Highly Sensitive Person: How to Thrive When the World Overwhelms You*, (Portland, OR; Broadway Books, 1997) p. 6.

6 *Ibid.*

7 Steven Covey, *The 7 Habits of Highly Effective People*, (New York; Free Press; 1990)

CHAPTER 7

MANAGING YOUR EMOTIONS

Managing your emotions is an inside job. That is why it is important to learn techniques to make attitude adjustments. You can then direct your emotions more efficiently. Happiness comes through emotions qualified by the heart.

—Doc Childre and Howard Martin

EMOTIONAL intelligence is not about becoming emotionless. As you build your emotional competencies, you will continue to experience the full spectrum of emotions. You will just be able to manage them better.

Managing your emotions entails plotting a course around or through them so that your final destination is a constructive one. For some, managing emotions is not easy, particularly when emotions are elevated. Here are some intrinsic qualities you can develop to effectively manage your emotions.

Self Discipline

There are times when you need to use self-regulation to react in a balanced way, and there are times when you need discipline and courage to respond in a more assertive or forceful manner. When applying self-discipline, it is very important that you think about the process and your desired outcome by asking yourself a series of questions. How should I react? Does the situation require force? What am I willing to lose? What can I gain if I handle this effectively? What is the right timing for a response? What do I want to achieve? Which approach should I use to attain my goals? Is there a secondary approach I can use if the primary one is ineffective? In reality, you may have seconds to give thought to your response and act; at other times, you may have days or weeks.

Commitment

Commitment is a characteristic that lies below the surface of self-discipline. Your values and beliefs are deeply embedded in your drive behind your commitment. Commitment varies from person to person, depending on your system of values. For instance, two students each received a scholarship to attend university. One was committed and driven to exceed, because she wants to be the first member of her family to obtain a degree. Her drive was intrinsic, and her focus was unwavering. The other student wanted to attend college, but her parents were pushing her to study law, which was of no interest to her. Her parents were both lawyers but she really wanted to study fine art. So the second student was less committed because her heart was not connected to her major.

> **commitment:** an agreement (verbal or written) or pledge to perform some action in the future.

Commitment to managing your emotions is a key to your success at work, school, and other relationships. Oriah Mountain Dreamer, in her poem, "The Invitation," says, "It doesn't interest me if the story you are telling me is true. I want to know if you can disappoint another to be true to yourself; if you can bear the accusation of betrayal and not betray your own soul."[1] This verse asserts that courage and commitment work together because the true test of commitment is what you do when you are facing a challenge.

Resilience

Resilience and commitment work together. Resilience undergirds commitment; it is the ability to maintain mental and emotional elasticity so that you can adapt to uncontrollable circumstances. It is about navigating unexpected twists and turns while not allowing your emotions to slow you down or cause you to give up. It is about seeing obstacles and failures as temporary or as learning tools instead of proof of impossibility. Optimism lies at the core of resilience.

> **resilience:** is the positive capacity of people to cope with stress and catastrophe. It also includes the ability to bounce back to homeostasis after a disruption.

Flexible Optimism

Optimism is not related to perceiving a utopian or perfect world. Utopian desires are more related to fantasy or delusion. Optimism is related to how you manage the emotions behind your perceptions so that your perceptions can empower you.

Martin Seligman describes a type of optimism that he calls "flexible optimism."[2] His position is that optimism isn't always appropriate. Instead, flexible optimism is a skill he uses when he needs to decide whether optimism is appropriate or a more realistic view. He recognizes that some situations are outside our control, but we can introduce flexibility that will allow us to remain empowered whether we are being optimistic or realistic. Flexible optimism is useful in managing your emotions, because there are times when you need to be honest with yourself and acknowledge the unthinkable, and still remain empowered despite the acknowledgment.

Tools for Managing Your Emotions

Now that we have explored a few characteristics of a person who can manage his emotions, let's explore various tools you can use to self-regulate.

Reframing

Most of us don't have the luxury of expressing elevated emotions whenever we want to. We need a tool we can use in the moment. One of the more powerful tools for self-management is reframing. A co-worker once shared a quote by Will Bowen, author of "Complaint-free Relationships; How to Positively Transform Your Personal, Work, and Love Relationships." with me. It was simply this, "Hurt people hurt people[3]." This is because they unconsciously project what they are feeling inwardly toward the people in their environments and leave a trail of emotional demolition. Reframing is necessary so you can learn to see that the perceived attack is not really about you, although your action may have triggered the reaction.

Another way you can reframe a situation is by learning to identify opportunities or the silver lining. If you are in an emotional state that does not allow you to perceive the opportunities in a situation, invite the input of a relative or friend who is not contaminated by your emotions. Your goal is to engage an external voice of reason until you can do this for yourself. There are people who view choices in terms of this or that. Another powerful reframing tool is to fight the need to choose one option or the other. Instead, we can creatively integrate both or multiple options into a solution. We will explore reframing again in Chapter 11.

Separating Your Emotions from Viral Emotions

This is especially useful for highly sensitive people because your emotional receptors can be overloaded. If you are a person who absorbs other people's emotive emissions like a sponge, it can be hard to determine which emotions are yours.

For many years, I faced this challenge. The primary way I separate my emotions is by using logic. For instance, if I am experiencing fear or anxiety that has nothing to do with my current reality, I ask myself if there are any perceivable or unconscious reasons why I should be experiencing fear or anxiety. If the answer is no, then there is a very good chance the emotion does not originate with me, even though it feels real. This process does not decrease the experience of heightened emotion, but it helps me make objective decisions.

Exposing Your Emotional Blind Spots

In biology, a blind spot is a place on the optic disc of the retina where there are no photoreceptor cells. The lack of photoreceptor cells is not registered, because the brain compensates by creating detail for the blind spot based on the information received by the other eye. In an emotional intelligence context, a blind spot is a behavior you cannot perceive that others can easily detect. With blind spots, your filters assign a different perspective to the behavior than the people experiencing the behavior, and their perception could be stifling your progress. In other words, your blind spot is an open secret, because it is in plain view for everyone to see, but you are unable to perceive it the same way as others.

To see your blind spot, you will need other eyes to fill in the interpretive differences. A skilled coach or mentor can act as a mirror to help you perceive your reputation or brand more clearly. Alternatively, you can improve your ability to decipher nonverbal communication, and this requires breaking out of your perception of yourself by seeking other views. If you seek input from the people close to you, be sure you are ready to receive information that is not aligned with your perception without being defensive.

Considering the Consequences of Your Actions

Consequential thinking is the process of considering various outcomes based on a decision. This type of thinking is based on your logic, critical thinking, empathy, and visualization skills. It considers multiple outcomes to determine which decision makes the most sense for you.

I can still remember one of the sayings of my principal at high school. She would always tell us, "You suffer or enjoy the consequences of your actions." I interpreted this at the time as you are rewarded or penalized based on your actions. Later in life, I realized I couldn't take a literal approach to this, as sometimes seemingly negative consequences end up having positive outcomes, and positive consequences can have negative outcomes. For example, someone once told me that rejection is a form of protection. Rejection seems like a negative consequence, but over time, you may recognize that the rejection protected you from an unwanted result.

There are people who are reactionary, hard to reason with, and sometimes dogmatic. Their reactions are often unconscious knee-jerk reactions. They are oblivious to their impact on others, and this can be a strain, because no one enjoys working with people who have no self-awareness or discipline. In fact, reactionary people can sometimes be perceived as abusive.

There are times when you respond after considering an appropriate response, but because your emotions are so elevated, your state of mind and emotions may cause you to disregard important facts or consequences. If you have the time, cool off. Your perspective may change after a cooling-off period.

Setting Clear Boundaries

If you allow people to encroach upon your boundaries, you can compromise your ability to grow and develop emotionally. Setting boundaries consciously is a three-step process. The first step is to identify the areas of your life that require boundaries. The second step is that once you identify these areas, decide what the boundary will be and what you are prepared to do to maintain it. Thirdly, always remember that setting boundaries is about continuously maintaining limits or controls, and you are always empowered with the right to say no!

Yielding

Yielding does not have to mean giving up your point. You may decide to yield to serve the greater good. Yielding is different from giving up because when you yield, you have not given up your power. You can still actively participate in creating the path of change.

I participated in a seminar where I witnessed a powerful exercise on yielding. Two participants were asked to stand back-to-back, linking arms. Each person was instructed to not allow the other person to push him or her in any direction. As instructed, both people applied equal resistance and neither moved in any direction.

> **Yielding:** a willingness to comply or submit to the requests of another. One can yield in a battle in order to win a war, so yielding does not have to imply giving up the vision.

When the volunteers were asked to stop resisting each other, they were asked to perform a second demonstration. While they were still back to back with arms linked, one person was asked to yield while the other pushed. What we realized then was the person who yielded was able to steer the person pushing in a desired direction harnessing and guiding the impetus. Seminar participants witnessing these two demonstrations realized that the person who yielded ended up leading the situation.

Early adopters are the first to yield and are usually leaders in any change circumstance. If you have the ability to perceive the positive consequences of change, adaptability may be effortless for you. Architects of change rely on early adopters to win over the others, because they become the authentic voice of support for the change.

The Benefits of Managing Your Emotions

Achievement Motivation

Bruce Tuckman, Dennis A. Abry, and Dennis R. Smith, authors of *Learning and Motivation Strategies: Your Guide to Success*, assert that achievement motivation is about attitude, drive, and strategy.[4] Your values, beliefs, and experiences form your attitude. Your drive is based on your desire, belief in yourself, and commitment to your desire.

For instance, you may want to make more money, but your fear of the unknown or of change is greater than your desire for more money. If you are facing similar circumstances, it is conceivable that you may become immobilized. A key element of achievement motivation is self-efficacy. Self-efficacy is your belief in your capability to achieve your goals and is directly linked to your intrinsic motivation, which is your ability to be motivated by your goals and values.

As an emotionally intelligent person, you are motivated by your purpose and self-efficacy. You are not swayed by external ideas or opinions, but you may adopt an external idea if the new idea introduces new, factual, and relevant information that adds a deeper perspective. The bottom line is that you did not change because of external pressure. Your internal cognitive process and commitment to your goals transformed your thinking.

Understanding Your Power

Lao Tzu, known as the Father of Taoism, once stated, "Knowing others is intelligence; knowing yourself is true wisdom. Mastering others is strength; mastering yourself is true power."[5]

In the 1940s, Abraham Maslow created a model called the "Four Stages of Learning" that illustrates how your learning can evolve over time. In applying it to emotional intelligence, ideally, you want to move from unconscious incompetence, where you have no control over your reactions and how they impact others, to a state of conscious incompetence, where you are aware of your emotions and building self-management skills.

As you practice your emotional competencies, you can move to conscious competence, where you consciously practice the skills you need to manage your emotions. At this level you still have to give your responses some thought. The ideal competence level to achieve is unconscious competence, which means that your new, emotionally responsible responses are now hardwired and have become second nature.

Impact and influence are very important and powerful competences that are useful to anyone. They refer to one's power to influence an outcome by using skills of negotiation, persuasion, curiosity and sometimes charm. If you are skilled at impact and influence, you can influence your peers, reporting officer or co-workers. Your status will not affect your power to influence others—your abilities will.

Successful influencers use their emotional intelligence to identify and communicate their emotions. By extension, these people are particularly skilled at reading the emotions of people around them. Based on my experiences, there is a fine line between influence and manipulation. So be sure not to allow your skills of impact and influence to mutate by applying pressure to people causing them to do things that violate their personal value systems. Influential people can possess formal or informal power within organizational structures, so their opportunity to influence is strong because they have a respected voice in group systems.

---

1 Oriah Mountain Dreamer, *The Invitation*, (New York; HarperCollins, 2006)

2 Martin Seligman. *Learned Optimism: How to Change Your Mind and Your Life,* (New York; A.A. Knopf, 1991)

3 Will Bowen. *Complaint Free Relationships; How to Positively Transform your Personal, Work, and Love Relationships.* (New York; Harmony, 2009)

4 Bruce Tuckman, Dennis Abry, and Dennis R. Smith, *Learning and Motivation Strategies: Your Guide to Success.* (Upper Saddle, New Jersey; Prentice Hall; 2 Edition, 2007)

5 Lao Tzu, *Tao Te Ching* (600 B.C.E.)

CHAPTER 8

LINKING EMOTIONAL INTELLIGENCE AND CRITICAL THINKING

Most simply, emotional intelligence can reasonably be conceived as a measure of the degree to which a person successfully (or unsuccessfully) applies sound judgment and reasoning to situations in the process of determining emotional or feeling responses to those situations. It would entail, then, the bringing of (cognitive) intelligence to bear upon emotions. It would encompass both positive and negative emotions.

—Linda Elder

DEVELOPING your critical thinking skills is yet another tool that complements the development of your emotional intelligence. Dr. Linda Elder asserted that "critical thinking provides the crucial link between intelligence and emotions in the emotionally intelligent person."[1]

Michael Scriven and Richard Paul defined critical thinking as, "that mode of thinking—about any subject, content, or problem—in which the thinker improves the quality of his or her thinking by skillfully taking charge of the structures inherent in thinking and imposing intellectual standards on them."[2] This reinforces the notion that self-regulation is necessary in the critical thinking process.

Daniel Goleman, author of *Emotional Intelligence*, once stated that you experience an emotion and then you think. He said, "The emotional mind is far quicker that the rational mind, springing into action without pausing even a moment to consider what it is doing. Its quickness precludes the deliberate, analytic reflection that is the hallmark of the thinking mind."[3] Unlike Goleman, Elder's position is that you cannot experience an emotion without an underlying thought, so her model suggests that thoughts are the catalysts for emotional experiences.

Whichever explanation you prefer, the underlying assumption is that thoughts are related to emotional responses. Goleman implied that our unconscious associations lead to conscious after-thought. Elder asserted that it is not possible to experience emotion without an underlying thought. With this in mind, it follows that developing your critical thinking skills can assist you with managing your associations and other thoughts so you can respond objectively, particularly in emotionally-charged situations.

In his report, *Critical Thinking: A Statement of Expert Consensus for Purposes of Educational Assessment and Instruction*, Dr. Peter A. Facione stated, "We understand critical thinking to be purposeful, self-regulatory judgment which results in interpretation, analysis, evaluation, and inference, as well as explanation of the evidential, conceptual, methodological, criteriological, or contextual considerations upon which that judgment is based. Critical thinking is essential as a tool of inquiry. As such, critical thinking is a liberating force in education and a powerful resource in one's personal and civic life."[4]

> **cognition:** cognitive mental processes. The rational activities of the mind. The part of mental functions that deals with logic, as opposed to affective, which deals with emotions.

Dr. Facione went on to say, "While not synonymous with good thinking, critical thinking is a pervasive and self-rectifying human phenomenon. The ideal critical thinker is habitually inquisitive, well-informed, trustful of reason, open-minded, flexible, fair-minded in evaluation, honest in facing personal biases, prudent in making judgments, willing to reconsider, clear about issues, orderly in complex matters, diligent in seeking relevant information, reasonable in the selection of criteria, focused in inquiry, and persistent in seeking results which are as precise as the subject and the circumstances of inquiry permit."[5]

Critical thinking can help you to look at your emotions at a root level. If you can reframe illogical, emotional, poorly informed, biased thoughts, you can neutralize your emotional triggers.

Cognition refers to your rational thinking process. This is where the critical thinking takes place, and if you have well-developed critical thinking skills, you will raise vital questions and concerns about your emotions and responses. Critical thinkers are open to other points of view and test their conclusions and the conclusions of others. As a critical thinker, you also identify relevant information and attempt to elucidate abstract information, transforming it into concrete ideas, solutions, or the right questions.

Some people trap themselves in an endless emotional loop, because they are not able to distinguish fact from the unsubstantiated. For instance, if a family member informs you that your sister is angry with you, you can choose to go into an emotional spiral of confusion, anger, or fear that feeds on itself, or you can choose not to enter the loop and attempt to get the facts.

Others resort to emotional and personal attacks if they do not have a grasp of the issues or facts. These people are unable or unwilling to process information objectively because of limited cognitive skills or excessive emotion, so the only tool they access in the heat of the moment is personal attack.

Here are five actions you can take to sharpen your critical thinking skills:

1. Define the problem
   - Extrapolate the facts
   - Understand assumptions
   - Identify your biases
   - Understand multiple points of view
2. Distinguish the relevant from irrelevant
3. Understand the reliability of the source
4. Achieve objectivity
5. Draw conclusions and create solutions

1. Define the Problem

Gather information about the problem by asking questions. Ask questions to develop an understanding through collating facts and sifting through the information to establish relevance. Once you define the problem, seek possible root causes and review the problem from various perspectives. Ask who or what is contributing to the root causes; if policies (formal or informal) and procedures are contributing to the issue, determine their effect. Find out who the stakeholders are and how they are contributing or how they are affected.

Extrapolate the facts

Probing is usually discussed in the context of listening, but at its core, it is a powerful fact-finding tool. Open probes are designed to obtain surplus information. They usually start with interrogative words, such as *how, why,* or *what.* Open probes provide both useful and irrelevant information, and it is up to the listener to make the distinction by asking closed probes.

Closed probes are designed to obtain specific information. They start with probing words, such as *do/does,* and *are/is.* They elicit yes or no responses or other one-word answers. Open and closed probes can uncover opinions, so you need to test the information by drilling deeper into an issue or idea with additional probes. Your ability to master the use of open and closed probes combined with your critical thinking skills can help you extrapolate relevant facts and possibly prevent you from making unnecessary emotional investments.

Symptoms of a problem can appear to be facts because of how the information is presented and this can draw us into an emotional reaction. The logic makes sense, the conviction of the presenter is palpable, and there may even be some semblance of facts mixed in with the opinions. Using probes can help us get to the root cause.

There is a difference between fact and opinion. A statement of fact outlines what actually happened and is typically supported with evidence. Biases, beliefs, and judgments, which cannot be proven, are the basis of opinions. The first step in exposing opinion is to ask a series of questions designed to undermine inherent biases and deliberate spin so you can discover the facts. This could include requests for statistical information or other provable data, such as e-mails, letters, signatures, metrics, or speaking directly with the people involved.

Introducing additional points of view to the process of extrapolating facts can bring additional complexity or clarity depending on the nature of the new information and your critical thinking skills. Ideally, new perspectives can add depth and breadth to the data collated, but there is the danger that too much information can be confusing. If your critical thinking skills are refined, you can navigate the superfluous information, make better decisions, or create holistic solutions.

Your emotions, biases, and assumptions may cause you to create inferences or illogical conclusions. If you can find someone capable of neutrality, you can seek his/her input or test your assumptions by listing your assumptions, encouraging intra- and intergroup debate, understanding stakeholders and factions among stakeholders, ranking assumptions, and determining whether the assumption is correct or incorrect by obtaining the facts.

There will be times when the facts cannot be obtained or easily interpreted. Try not to delay your decision until you have all the information you think you need. Sometimes it is necessary to weigh the pros and cons of your decision to wait versus taking action, especially when you are emotional or if there is a crisis. Not making a decision is a decision to do nothing, and avoidance is sometimes not constructive or optimal.

Understand your assumptions

Review your assumptions, and if possible, attempt to understand the assumptions of the people communicating with you. Assumptions can be used in predictive circumstances, but in a predictive context, assumptions are researched. Assumptions made in problem solving circumstances can be based on insufficient data and individual filters built by your life experiences. So once you identify your assumptions, test them for factual content. If you detect opinion, seek to supplant it with facts where possible.

Identify your biases

I sometimes use an activity in my workshops called the "Halo or the Horn" exercise. The first step is to create a list of halo items: a list of the characteristics of people you are comfortable being around or people you prefer as colleagues. Then the participants are asked to compile a horn list, which consists of people they work with but find challenging.

The next step is to take the halo and horn lists and record the characteristics of the people listed. The two lists are designed to reveal the positive and negative biases held by participants. These biases can lead to behaviors that exclude and create emotions associated with rejection. In the workplace, unbridled positive biases lead to the formation of an exclusive group of employees who are highly favored by management. Conversely, unchecked negative biases can lead to the exclusion of the underperformers or co-workers who speak their minds regardless of the outcome.

Biases can drive judgments that can lead to misplaced or inappropriate emotions, so it is important to review the biases about which you are conscious and seek to uncover biases you unconsciously programmed as default positions.

Understand Multiple Points of View

Some people are very skilled at perceiving the world in black or white terms—a kind of binary scale. You decide that if it is not one thing, it must be the other. You perceive things as good or bad, right or wrong, fast or slow—you get the picture. When in a fundamentalist mode, your assumptions are based on your biases and the limited option(s) you are able to perceive.

In reality, there are many colors in the spectrum and understanding this will help you to perceive more than two possible points of view when considering a situation.

2. Distinguish the Relevant from Irrelevant

As part of the critical thinking process, you will need to be able to distinguish between relevant and irrelevant information. There are times when emotion introduces irrelevant information and opinions that appear to be relevant or even factual. It is important to make a distinction here. The information may be relevant to the person experiencing emotions because of their filters, but the information may also be confusing the issues.

Opinions are opinions if they are not provable, so always remember to ask questions to test for assumptions, biases, and overriding emotion, because it is usually difficult to remain objective in a heightened, emotive state.

A process of separating fact from opinion should help you identify which information is relevant to the problem. If you disregard an issue or opinion as irrelevant, but it is important to the person experiencing emotion, you may derail the process of finding a solution. Identifying the real issues for clarity and problem solving is a balanced and fair approach. But before issues can be resolved, the source of emotion needs to be addressed.

3. Understand the Reliability of the Source

Give some thought to the person providing you with information and ask yourself why he is sharing this information with you. Is it possible that the messenger has a self-serving agenda or motive? You need to understand his biases, loyalties, critical thinking skills, and objectives. Allowing people to give you information that pushes your buttons will ignite intense emotions within you. By understanding the reliability of your source, you can avoid being manipulated by others.

4. Achieve Objectivity

If you are in a state of intense positive or negative emotion, you can take steps to relax, so you can separate your emotion from the thinking process. Some people use breathing techniques to regulate themselves, some count to ten, others talk it through with a trusted listener, and some take a walk. Whatever your process for diffusing your emotions, take the time to calm down, because you do not want your emotions to lead you to a decision that you will regret because of impaired objectivity.

Diana Mertz Hsieh describes objectivity as "a method of acquiring knowledge by reasoning solely based on the facts of reality and in accordance with the laws of logic."[6] An emotionally intelligent person seeks to balance objectivity with managing emotions. Otherwise, you will be perceived as detached or impersonal. E.Q. Librium seekers focus on connection and heart.

5. Draw Conclusions and Create Solutions

It is time to make a decision. At this point in the critical thinking process, you will need to decide on a solution or a course of action based on the researched and processed information. It is easy to be stuck at this point when you have irrelevant information and heightened emotions. If you are in a state of indecision, the value system of your coworkers or your employer can give you clues about your next steps. In making your decision, you will need to understand the value and goal hierarchies as they relate to the situation and the key stakeholders. More specifically, you will need to identify the primary value and goal drivers of the people involved and use this information to move toward a conclusion.

Conclusions are not necessarily absolute or final.New information can modify your conclusions. Some people wait until they get all the information they need to draw a conclusion and create a solution. This is not always optimal, so inferences need to be made where facts are not available.

Drawing conclusions presupposes employment of the elements of critical thinking: problem identification, extrapolating the facts, understanding your assumptions, achieving objectivity, and identifying the reliability of the source all contribute to the conclusion and decision-making processes. It is important to understand the significance of emotions in critical thinking as emotions can thwart the process if they are not effectively navigated or harnessed.

---

[1] Elder, Linda "Cognition and Affect: Critical Thinking and Emotional Intelligence," in *Inquiry: Critical Thinking Across the Disciplines,* Winter, 1996. Vol. XVI, No. 2.

2 A statement by Michael Scriven & Richard Paul, *Defining Critical Thinking.* for the 8th Annual International Conference on Critical Thinking and Education Reform, Summer 1987.

3 Daniel Goleman, *Emotional Intelligence: Why It Can Matter More Than IQ,* (New York; Bantam Dell, 1st Edition; 1997) p.291.

4 Peter A. Facione, *Critical Thinking: A Statement of Expert Consensus for Purposed of Educational Assessment and Instruction,* (Milbrae, CA; California Academic Press, 1990) p. 2.

5 *Ibid.*

6 Diana Mertz Hsieh, "What is Objectivity?" in the 1999 article by Diana Metrz Hsieh, accessed December 2009, http://enlightenment.supersaturated.com/essays/text/dianamertzhsieh/objectivity.html.

CHAPTER 9

PURPOSE AND EMOTIONAL INTELLIGENCE

Except for the financially desperate, people do not work for money alone. What also fuels their passion for work is a larger sense of purpose or passion. Given the opportunity, people gravitate to what gives them meaning, to what engages their fullest commitment, talent, energy, and skill. That can mean changing jobs to get a better fit with what matters to us.

—Daniel Goleman

FOR some, passion, purpose, or voice is vague and unarticulated. You experience it as a feeling or a knowing. You probably know what you do not want to do or you know some things you do well, but you do not know how to bring all this information together so you can mobilize yourself on your journey of purpose.

Lights On, Lights Off

The first step in seeking your purpose is to discover what lights you up. Your lights are the twinkle in your eyes and the excitement or joy that emanates from you uncontrollably when you talk about your purpose. You automatically smile when you talk about your purpose. You can't help it, because you go to that deep place of flow, lights, and natural being by just thinking about it. Counselors and coaches are trained to observe your body and verbal language to find clues about what lights you up.

An indicator that someone is not yet attuned to their purpose is when they are asked what lights them up, and they answer by looking upward to the right, accessing the depths of their left brain, completely missing the answer in their hearts. If you are attempting to access your cognitive faculties to answer the question about your lights, you need to understand the true answer is not in your head; instead, you will have to access your heart intelligence.

Knowing what lights you up is sometimes not enough information to find your purpose. It may only be a piece of the mosaic that represents your purpose, because your lights may be ignited by more than one activity.

Finding Your Purpose: Lights On - Lights Off

Lights Off	Controlled Demotivated Disengaged Automatic Pilot
Lights On	Passionate Engaged Internally Motivated Empowered Focused

Figure 9.1: Finding Your Purpose.
Source: © 2011. Organizational Soul, Ltd.

Figure 9.1 shows what happens when your lights are on or off. When your lights are off, you feel controlled or stuck. You may be doing what someone else suggested, or you may be working because you need the money.

When your lights are off, the motivation to complete the duties outlined on your job description is not coming from your heart. It may be coming from the fear of losing your job. People whose lights are off don't feel like going to work or are not fully engaged. There are some people whose lights are off who are in the right profession but feel they have no voice.

Conversely, when your lights are on and you are in a supportive environment, you are engaged, your passion is ignited, your creativity is flowing, and time disappears, because you are so absorbed in what you are doing. You are motivated internally by what you know to be your purpose, and you are empowered.

I have a client who found a job that completely lights him up, but his co-workers are caustic, toxic, undermining, and negative. He chooses to remain in the environment because the opportunity to do what he loves outweighs the effects of contaminated environment. He maintains that this is the best job of his career. Unlike my client, there are others who place high value on working in an environment that is respectful and supportive; it is all a personal choice.

As previously stated, finding your purpose is a critical component of helping you manage or even nullify emotions that are unproductive for you. For example, you may be in a state of frustration, feeling trapped in a dead-end job with no perceived room to grow. This can generate feelings of disappointment, unfulfillment, or failure. On the other hand, you may love what you do but you don't enjoy working with your co-workers. Whatever your challenge, when you uncover your purpose, those challenges will not seem insurmountable. You will find yourself being more tolerant, empowered, or able to perceive and make choices.

The Path to Purpose

Here are a few considerations you can explore once you determine your purpose.

Determine the Right Relationships for You

Ask yourself what the right relationships are so you can determine whether you have outgrown your current relationships or network. Relationships can be personal and familial, relate to your current or future career, or relate to your hobbies or interests. No matter the type of relationship you are considering, think about creating and cultivating relationships that will support you on your path, present opportunities or ones that will help you to be open to change when you need to be. You can also think about letting go of relationships that are unsupportive or toxic and embrace relationships with people who have achieved what you want to accomplish.

Focus on Your Potential

There are many ways to learn a new skill. There is the beaten path, where you can opt to attend seminars and conferences or participate in online courses. You can also volunteer your time to do something that lights you up. Most times, this option is disregarded because volunteering takes time, and there is no initial financial reward. This is a shortsighted approach because volunteering can be one of the most rewarding networking experiences you can choose.

Some people enrich their lives and careers by relationships with mentors. Mentors don't usually seek you, so if you adopt the path of a life-long learner, you can identify mentors, volunteer to work with them, and ask them to help you to continuously seek new ways to stretch and edify yourself.

If you are an employee and choose to remain one, ask yourself whether the person responsible for leading your team and evaluating you is capable of seeing the highest version of you. If not, you may not be in the right environment for your purposeful development. You could end up being relegated to a biased version of you that is constricting and inferior to your potential. I have said this several times already because it is so important: if you are suffocated by your environment but love what you do, find the right environment, because you deserve to blossom.

Take Deliberate Steps in the Direction of Your Goals

Once you find your purpose, identify and take steps toward your goals by creating an action plan. The best pace is your natural pace. If you perceive that someone achieved more in their lives than you, you may be putting pressure on yourself that could cause you to cut corners. Avoid the trap of comparing yourself to others. Their goals are not your goals; their skills and resources are also very different from yours.

Create or Update Your Action Plan

Once some people have an idea of their purpose, they start "winging it" without an action plan. While winging it and ad-libbing may work, and opportunities may meet you in a state of readiness, codifying your thoughts into an action plan can help you take a focused, disciplined, and thoughtful approach that can pay off in the long term.

If you already have an action plan for your career and life and it is no longer relevant, you need to update it. For instance, Martha enjoyed selling silver jewelry, so she started a business with a partner. Over time, Martha realized her partner was not a good match. They had different value systems, so they mutually agreed to go into separate businesses. When they decided on separate businesses, it was necessary for Martha to update her plans, because she was faced with additional operational costs and other responsibilities that she did not factor into the original plan.

Mobilize Your Plan

It takes vision, focus, discipline, and courage to do what you believe is right for you. Mahatma Gandhi once said, "First they ignore you, then they laugh at you, then they attack you, and then you win." Mobilizing your plan may lead to unexpected objections, but always remember the obvious: you have to live with your decisions. So, if mobilizing your plan is the right thing to do because you are on purpose and the timing is right, step outside the boundaries of your comfort zone and the comfort zones other people have constructed for you.

Remember, you do not need to have a complete plan before you take action. Some people are taught that an action plan has to be perfected before getting started. This belief system can lead to inaction, because there are infinite opportunities to analyze and correct an action plan before it is executed.

I have learned that once you get started, things will go wrong anyway, because you can't think of every possible scenario. Learn to let go of your fears of the unknown, or of missing something or of things going wrong, and just get started. Sharpening your skill of adaptability will help you manage the process. It also gives you the opportunity to work on improving the self-regulation skills that will help you to manage your emotions when complications occur.

Don't be deterred by obstacles. Setbacks happen to everyone, but not everyone is capable of overcoming them. Remember, there is always another way, time, or opportunity, and all you need to do is possess the vision and have the optimism and stamina to make it happen.

Break Your Plan into Small Steps

It is easy to feel overwhelmed when you know where you want to go, and the path is unclear. One way you can make your plan less daunting is to set deadlines that can be broken into small segments. This will give you the small wins you need to bolster your confidence and keep you on track.

Build Your Support Team

Most successful people are surrounded by a team. They progress based on having the right people working with them. Networks that can provide you with support are built through social media, professional groups, past professional relationships, clubs, or friends. Additionally, there are coaches for every imaginable area of your life and career, including business coaches, leadership coaches, nutrition and health coaches, life coaches, et cetera. I suggest that if you can, pay for the services you need, because if you do not pay it is possible that you will not get the level of service you deserve.

Conduct Your Research and Embrace New Ideas and Technology

Your area of interest may be evolving and expanding. Research and learn as much as you can so you can be relevant and up-to-date. Preparation can help to shorten the time it takes to master a new role, and it can put you in a very competitive position.

From a technology standpoint, be sure your technological competencies align with your aspirations. For instance, there is no point in wanting to be an administrative assistant when you are not proficient with word processing, creating presentations, or developing spreadsheets.

Be Wary of Naysayers and Dream Stealers

These people have a knack for telling you all the wonderful things you cannot do. Their arguments may be rational and true but you can overcome them, so use discernment. Instead of entertaining naysayers who put your lights out, surround yourself with people who sincerely support your creativity through balanced feedback.

One of my mentors once told me that courage is about experiencing fear and doing the things you fear despite the effect the emotion is having on you. Following your purpose can cause you to face ridicule or anger. Remain on your path, because the transformative power of purpose is inevitable if you can manage to get past the attacks.

Reinvent Yourself

Reinvention sounds simpler than it is. It assumes you know yourself and what you want to change. It also assumes you have a vision for yourself. Sometimes the changes you need to make will be subtle, and other times the changes will be dramatic and involve both internal and external makeovers. Writer Susan Crandell once said, "Let go of the old life to reach for the new life, and trust yourself that it will be there."[1] Reinvention is about possessing the confidence to face your old view of yourself and to let it go so the enhanced version of you can materialize.

Build Your Personal Brand

In an article in the August 1997 edition of *Fast Company*, author Tom Peters, wrote, "We are CEOs of our own companies: Me Inc. To be in business today, our most important job is to be head marketer for the brand called You."[2]

Your personal brand is a unique proposal of value that differentiates you from others. When you brand yourself personally you communicate a message of differentiation that represents the skills you would like to publicize based on your goals.

Dan Schawbel, author of *Me 2.0: Building a Powerful Brand to Achieve Career Success*, asserts "Personal branding consists of three elements:

- Value Proposition: What do you stand for?
- Differentiation: What makes you stand out?
- Marketability: What makes you compelling?"[3]

When you start moving along your path to purpose, people will recognize your lights, and it is up to you to deliberately develop your brand whether you are an employee or entrepreneur. If you have a personal branding strategy, you should remain aligned with your strategy, as inconsistency will lead to ineffective branding. Your goal should be to do things on your terms, not because someone asked you. Otherwise, you can end up with boundary issues that negatively impact your ability to execute your branding strategy.

Here are the steps you can take to develop a personal brand based on Hubert Rampersad's Model of Authentic Branding found in *Effective Personal and Company Brand*:[4]

- Create personal vision and mission statements. A personal vision statement is a statement of a desired future state. A personal mission statement is a statement of your priorities and values in the present.
- Complete a SWOT analysis for yourself indicating your strengths, weaknesses, opportunities, and threats.
- Then create a plan focused on developing relevant skill deficiencies, setting branding goals and measurements that will define success for you.
- Then execute your plan.

Building a personal branding strategy is directly linked to the emotional intelligence competence of identifying your purpose and setting goals to bring your purpose into reality. Purpose-driven people experience the full spectrum of their emotions. They feel the highs as intensely as the lows, yet they are still creative, engaged, and driven.

1 Susan Crandell, *Thinking about Tomorrow: Reinventing Yourself at Midlife*, (New York; Grand Central Publishing, July 2009).

2 Tom Peters, "The Brand Called You," Fast Company, August 1997.

3 Dan Schawbel, *Me 2.0: Build a Powerful Brand to Achieve Career Success*, (New York; Kaplan, 2009).

4 Hubert Rampersad, *Authentic Personal and Company Brand Management: A New Blueprint for Building and Aligning a Powerful Leadership Brand*, (North Carolina; Information Age Publishing, 2008).

CHAPTER 10

EMOTIONAL INTELLIGENCE AND VALUE SYSTEMS

Values give meaning to people's lives. Organizational performance is directly related to its ability to tap into its human potential. For many people, work is one of the most important ways they are able to give expression to who they are in their search for fulfillment. When a person works for a firm whose values mirror those of their own, they will respond by fulfilling their potential and tapping into their deepest levels of creativity.

—Vadim Kotelnikov

WHEN I learned that emotional intelligence is not about being nice, I narrowly interpreted it to mean if you are emotionally intelligent, you can stand in your power respectfully, not letting anyone cross personal boundaries. It didn't occur to me at the time that it could also mean that you could use your emotional intelligence to create a state of confusion within your environment. This is when I started to explore the connections between value systems and emotional intelligence. Your value and belief systems drive how you use your emotional intelligence, no matter your level of mastery of the competencies.

Value Systems

In relationships, value system alignment is essential for emotional balance, whether you are relating to an individual a group, or an organization. For example, if two people are friends, and they both say they value honesty, but one person's actions start to demonstrate deep dishonesty, there will be dissonance. This may be reconcilable, but if not, the emotional betrayal may create an irreparable situation.

As an employee, it is essential for your value system to be aligned with the value system of your employer if you want to avoid any value-based conflict. When there is incongruence, there is a higher likelihood of negative emotion.

CASE STUDY #9: Patrice and Mandy

Value systems vary depending on a person and a situation. For example, Patrice and Mandy are friends who work in different departments for the same employer. They are both heads of departments and are competing to attract the same staff member to their respective departments. Both managers need a results-driven team player so they can achieve their goals. Patrice thought Mandy could be trusted, so she described the candidate to Mandy, and even shared the salary offer, not realizing that Mandy was also targeting the same employee for a vacancy in her department.

Mandy never disclosed that she was also interested in attracting the candidate and used the information to make a better offer. The candidate accepted Mandy's offer, and Patrice was devastated when she learned of the decision. She was shocked that Mandy appeared to value winning the recruitment competition more than their working relationship and friendship. For someone like Mandy, friendships may be important, but they shift in value given a change in circumstances. Depending on a person's value system, factors such as status, compensation, and power can override the value of friendships.

Constructive Emotional Intelligence

When you intend to use emotional intelligence to benefit yourself and others, here are value-based characteristics you can develop that can lead to constructive outcomes for you and the people around you. Keep in mind that some of these traits are ineffective in highly political environments that value form over substance.

1. Integrity
2. Situational ethics
3. Ownership
4. If you say you are going to do something, do it!
5. Recognize biases
6. Demonstrate courage
7. Weigh as many sides as possible
8. Forgiveness
9. Communication
10. Responsiveness and resourcefulness

CASE STUDY #10: Camille's New Job

Camille decided to join ABC Company twelve months ago because she was promised training opportunities and interesting work. Training was her highest value, because while she enjoyed interesting work with her previous employer, she believed her skills were not being developed. After Camille joined her new employer, she realized she had been duped. The work was engaging, as in her last job, but she realized her new employers had no intention of investing in her development. In fact, the company did not seem to value training—their focus was only on results.

When she started her new job, Camille's emotions were excitement and anticipation. After twelve months, however, her excitement changed to frustration, betrayal, and anger, so she soon found a new job and resigned, because she did not want to work for a company that lacked integrity.

---

1. Integrity

Integrity is inextricably linked to trust, and trust is the foundation that undergirds the activities and interactions of a functional, well-adjusted team. When trust is absent, people typically become suspicious or guarded about one another. When trust is present, members of the team are open, participative, engaged, and willing to be vulnerable.

Integrity is about aligning your values and actions. Being able to remain in integrity takes effort and courage in some environments or situations because you run the risk of being isolated for standing up for your beliefs.

2. Situational Ethics

Sometimes people who want to remain in integrity are faced with the option of breaking the rules. Joseph Fletcher, an Episcopal priest and author of the situational ethics model[1] asserts that moral principles can sometimes be relaxed if love is best served. From my perspective, love can also refer to the greater good. Based on my understanding, this model does not suggest that we should cast out all morality, because there is definitely a place for it.

To illustrate his theory, Father Fletcher enumerated a story about a woman who was separated from her husband and children and sent to a Russian prisoner of war camp. The only way she could save her own life (i.e., be released to her home country and find her family) was to become pregnant. With this knowledge, the woman asked a guard to impregnate her, and he did. This decision saved her life, and eventually she was able to locate and reunite with her family.

Whether you agree with Fletcher and his philosophy of situational ethics, it happens in everyday life. It is sometimes rejected as a viable option, because it blurs your perceived absolute values of right and wrong. Another reason for rejection is that this form of ethics can be abused if applied inappropriately. So if situational ethics does not appeal to you, use another approach.

> **situational ethics:** a Christian ethical theory that was principally developed in the 1960s by the Episcopal priest, Joseph Fletcher. It basically states that sometimes other moral principles can be cast aside in certain situations if love is best served.

3. Ownership

Blaming others for your shortcomings appoints fault or responsibility to someone else in an effort to distract attention from your culpability. Blame slows down the decision-making process as the issue degenerates into finding out whose fault it is instead of finding out the cause, what went wrong, or how it can be fixed.

Blame is an obvious self-preservation tactic based on fear. Blame can be used to cover up your incompetence or an oversight, because you are afraid of being exposed, judged, embarrassed, or attacked. Blamers prefer deflecting rather than accountability. In a constructive emotional intelligence environment, there is a focus on facts instead of emotions. Blamers can be short-circuited by team leaders who facilitate a conversation based on integrity and accountability.

4. If You Say You Are Going to Do Something, Do It!

If you agree to take action, you may have agreed because you do not want to appear to be resisting the person who made the request even though you really don't agree with the action. Some of us follow through with our commitment despite our internal disagreement. Others agree and do nothing, because either they chose a path of passive aggression, or they are afraid to admit they don't know how. No matter the reason, if you don't follow through on your commitments, there can be consequences. An obvious consequence of not following through is that you can be labeled as lazy, unproductive, incompetent, disorganized, or passive aggressive. As you will notice, none of these labels lend themselves to consideration for a promotion.

Whether anger or fear is driving your decision not to keep your word, you can seek to overcome these emotions by reviewing the consequences of your inaction.

Considering the consequences of your inaction is important, because not doing something you committed to do will erode trust in you. If you choose to take a more constructive path, you will have to face your emotions of fear or anger and take appropriate corrective steps.

5. Recognize Biases

Learn to recognize your biases so you can determine when you are responding to facts and when you are responding to your prejudices. Insist on finding the facts by asking yourself questions designed to get past your preconceived notions.

Sometimes people give you intentionally manipulative advice. Other times, their opinions are inaccurate. Hold them to the same standard as you hold yourself. Be consistent about finding the facts by asking questions designed to extrapolate provable details.

6. Demonstrate Courage

There will always be someone who disagrees with your decision, so always ensure your decisions are aligned with your goals and values. When you are making a decision for a group, always remember to weigh as many perspectives as possible, because the extra points of view can lead to a more effective, and holistic solution or response.

7. Weigh as Many Sides as Possible

Attempting to identify and weigh as many sides of a situation as possible is part of the critical-thinking process, and it starts with identifying the stakeholders and possible outcomes of decisions. This will help you think through the consequences of your actions and prevent you from focusing on emotions. One caution in weighing the sides of a situation is to avoid letting your biases influence the weight you place on any perspective.

8. Forgiveness

Jen is a manager and was invited to a meeting to provide input into a decision about the career of one of her direct reports. At the meeting, she recounted a mistake the employee made ten years ago, indicating it may make him unsuitable for the position.

If you are in a similar situation, you should ask yourself a few questions to test for objectivity and forgiveness. Is it fair to still hold the employee accountable for a mistake made ten years ago? Is this information still relevant? Has he maintained appropriate behaviors since the mistake? What current evidence supports allowing your out-of-date information to enter the decision-making process? If there is no evidence, it may be time for you to let go of your limiting bias, forgive the error, and give the employee a chance. Keep in mind that the lack of relevant data to support your point of view can also create biases against you.

Forgiveness is about letting go of the past to plot a new course for the future. Forgiveness is powerful, because it allows healing by providing opportunities for people to redeem themselves. Sometimes I hear people say, "I will forgive, but I won't forget." Forgiveness should not be confused with lowering your boundaries to the point where they can be trampled again.

Healthy boundaries should be established when forgiving someone, and healthy boundaries should exist in any relationship. If you have lost trust in a person, boundaries will shift to accommodate the new information. For instance, if a friend betrays you and you forgive her, but the trust is gone, it takes behavioral consistency and time to re-establish trust. During the trust-building process, modified boundaries should be set, and this could mean different things depending on the people involved.

9. Communication

We always hear the word *communication,* and it can mean so many things. Sometimes I observe managers who do not provide necessary updates to their support staff; they expect their team to notice or know what they are doing, not realizing members of their team are most likely focused on other things.

Information dissemination is a two-sided responsibility. Both the transmitter and receiver are responsible for ensuring clarity. There are times members of a team refrain from asking important questions, because they do not want to seem incompetent. As a result, a channel of relevant communication is closed, and a communication gap is created. Communication gaps cause emotion to build, because the lack of communication leads to an environment of mistrust.

The most effective leaders inform the appropriate people about what is happening at the right time. They ensure there are healthy flows of information both vertically (top down and bottom up), horizontally, and diagonally if the environment is open to this.

10. Responsiveness and Resourcefulness

Understanding priorities and responding in a timely fashion are traits that I observe in team players. They understand interconnectivity and the consequences of action and inaction for themselves and members of the team. People with emotional intelligence who are not team players may also understand interconnectivity and the consequences of their actions.

There are times when you are expected to perform but do not have the resources. Some people let their anger, hopelessness, or fear immobilize them; others navigate their emotions and make situations work by getting creative about locating the resources they need.

Emotions can surface when someone challenges your values, so if you value collaboration, balance, forgiveness, communication, responsiveness, fairness, and accountability, emotional intelligence can help you to mitigate the risks of negative long-term consequences.

1 Joseph Fletcher, *Situation Ethics*, (Calgary, AB; Canadian Institute for Law, Theology, and Public Policy, 1999).

PART TWO

ACHIEVING E.Q. LIBRIUM

CHAPTER 11

GETTING UNSTUCK

Motivation gives the first push, but you need persistence and self- discipline to get to the finish line.

—Remez Sasson

TO achieve a state of being unstuck, become conscious of your limiting thought patterns and emotions. Here are some actions you can take to get unstuck and move your career along your desired path.

Avoid saying "I am too busy"

The logic behind this reason is understandable. You are probably very busy, so you don't have the time to write and execute an action plan for your career. I used to say I was too busy, because I was very busy during the day and too tired in the evenings to focus on my personal goals. I was frustrated and feeling I was in an infinite loop of tasks. Then one day I decided to resign from a company where I had spent almost two decades.

When we say we are too busy it means we are too busy to plan for our personal development and execute that plan. Planning is an essential part of getting unstuck, so I support getting started with a business plan template or a career development plan. While I do support planning wholeheartedly, it is not always necessary to have a full plan in place to get started.

You may feel the opportune time to make a career move will magically materialize, and your circumstances will change, allowing you to do what you need to do. This is disempowered, unrealistic thinking, and it contributes to keeping you stuck. Planning takes time, and if the real reason you are stuck is that you do not know what you want to do, explore your purpose and start a plan. If you allow yourself to be distracted by busyness, the change you dream about may not materialize.

Open the Doors Yourself

Waiting passively for doors to open is another obstacle to a purpose-driven existence. Be clear about the reason you want to wait, because if you want a promotion and you wait for it to happen, you may not get what you want. For instance, I have observed that some people wait and finally receive a promotion they did not want. Others wait and get promoted, because they were the best person who applied for the position but not necessarily the best person for the job.

Sometimes very competent employees decide to wait, but a co-worker who is more political or visible may maneuver to get ahead of them. So, while patience can be an admirable quality, the wisdom to know whether or not you should be patient with your current employer is essential.

Set Your Boundaries

Many people get stuck because saying no is not part of their vocabulary. Some get overloaded with work because they have not developed the skill of negotiating deadlines with their reporting manager. Others are stuck because they are part of a gossip network, and the negative information they receive cripples their progress as a result of their reactions.

Recognize Limiting Patterns

It is hard to perceive your behaviors clearly if they are unconsciously programmed. One way to detect your patterns and get unstuck is to observe how people react to you. This is not a foolproof tool because so many things trigger different people, but it can be an indicator, particularly if you notice a pattern of responses to your behavior.

Another way to detect patterns that are impeding your emotional evolution is to observe your emotions and your corresponding behaviors. Do you withdraw in fear or do you fight? Some people go into denial and prefer to stick their heads in the sand. There are numerous patterns that can limit you, so learn to watch your patterns so you can consciously choose appropriate reactions.

Maslow's Hierarchy of Needs

Maslow's Hierarchy of Needs is a psychological model that illustrates what motivates us at various levels of our personal evolution. It is derived from Abraham Maslow's 1943 paper "A Theory of Human Motivation."

An understanding of your needs and motivation is necessary for emotional discipline because when your needs are not being met, emotions can emerge, and emotions such as fear, anger, frustration, anxiety, and hopelessness can cause you to feel stuck.

Maslow's Hierarchy of Needs

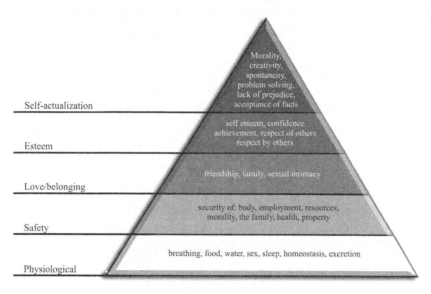

Figure 11.1: Maslow's Hierarchy of Needs.
Maslow, Abraham, "A Theory of Human Motivation." Psychological Review, #50 (1943) p370-396. Publisher: American Psychological Association, adapted with permission.

Getting unstuck is based on your ability to navigate your emotions when your needs are not being met at any one of the levels in Maslow's Hierarchy of

Needs illustrated in Figure 11.1. For instance, there are times when you may want your needs to be met at the self-actualization level, but your needs at the safety and security level are not being met. This forces you to focus on the lower level needs when you may prefer to be focused on self-actualizing activities.

CASE STUDY #11: Shane is Feeling Stuck

Shane was highly respected in international professional circles but not by his employers. His employers acknowledged the fact that his technical competencies were unrivaled, but his behaviors were perceived as confrontational and relentless. He wants to self-actualize, but he is forced to dwell between the levels of belonging and esteem building, because management does not respect him, nor does he respect them. When he digs his heels in, he is passionate about his position, and it has the effect of creating an opposing response that becomes a power struggle. As a result, his manager repeatedly ignored his projects and ideas, and consequently, his work was not effecting deeply needed changes. In other words, his ideas and work were ostracized, and this put him in a frustrating position of being stuck.

Shane chose not to utilize skills such as interest-based negotiation or political savvy that could have helped him communicate differently and gain acceptance for his ideas. He was so determined to get his point across that his ideas were rejected purely based on the approach or anticipated approach. Developing the emotional intelligence competence of consequential thinking can help Shane to think of alternative strategies for getting his work adopted and implemented while adhering to his values.

According to Innocent Mwangi, "The longer it takes to acquire certain habits, the more difficult it is to break them."[1] So be patient with yourself as you create new habits. It takes time to move from unconscious incompetence to unconscious competence.

Conquer Patterns of Low Self-Esteem

Nathaniel Branden once stated that "people of high self-esteem are not driven to make themselves superior to others; they do not seek to prove their value by measuring themselves against a comparative standard. Their joy is being who they are, not in being better than someone else."[2]

Low self-esteem is a pattern that creates the feeling of being stuck, because it generates a sense of powerlessness. There are times when it is useful to undergo a therapeutic process with a trained professional to uncover what is behind your limiting self-esteem patterns. Other times all you need is a coach or mentor who can help you identify your purpose and hold you accountable for achieving your goals.

Here are a few examples of how low self-esteem can manifest at work:

1. Supervisors not showing newcomers the ropes for fear of being displaced
2. Adopting a "Nobody likes me" attitude
3. Staying "under the radar" by putting on an "invisibility cloak"
4. Pretending to be someone you are not
5. Lying, blaming, and making excuses
6. Arrogance
7. The silent treatment

If you see yourself in any of these actions, take a step back and consider whether you need support, and if so, determine what type of help is best for you. A coach, counselor, or therapist can help you build your esteem. This is especially important if you don't want to get stuck in the self-esteem level of Maslow's Hierarchy of Needs.

Create Tolerance for Risk

In Maslow's Hierarchy of Needs, safety and security are higher than physiological needs. People who are risk averse can get stuck in either of these two levels because of their fears of failure, loss of income, or the unknown.

CASE STUDY #12: Lisa Takes a Risk

When Lisa completed her graduate studies, she thought she would take a job until she could determine what she wanted to do.

About ten years later, Lisa moved through the ranks of the company, and one day, she realized that this was supposed to be a temporary job. Ten years later, she was still there but still no closer to taking the steps she needed to resign.

Then one day she had a death in the family that totally shifted her perception of her life and career. She decided that it was time to take the risk. Lisa knew that once she was doing what she enjoyed, things would be difficult at times, but she was confident that she would succeed. So, she plotted a new course for herself.

For ten years, Lisa put safety and security above her deeper need to follow her path to purpose. While she was performing satisfactorily for her employer, she was not obtaining satisfaction from her work. Her risk aversion kept her supplanted in a reality where she was guaranteed a salary but felt like she was selling her soul until she had the impetus she needed to step into the unknown and be true to herself. This moved her through the self-esteem level of Maslow's model to the level of self-actualization.

Create Your Vision and Mission

While I mentioned action planning in an earlier chapter, it is also relevant here, because a plan can help to move you into action. Fear of the unknown tends to make risks seem larger than life. Whether you want to change your career or stay with your existing employer, create a plan that puts you in the driver's seat. Before creating your plan, set aside time for introspection. Consider these elements for your plan:

1. Create a vision for your life so you can visualize where you want to be in your personal life and career.

2. Create a personal mission statement that will serve as a statement of purpose in the present.

3. Define your core values and competencies, and identify environments that contribute best to your growth and development.

4. Create an action plan outlining what you want to do, and include relevant timelines and priorities. Your plan should include educational and experiential goals, and it should achieve balance between work, family, and play.

Put a Stop to It

In the context of Maslow's Hierarchy of Needs, knowing when to quit requires understanding when you pass the point of diminishing return. This may mean that you are taking blows to your self-esteem, and you need to make a decision that will help you to rebuild your esteem. Self-esteem and intrinsic motivation are linked, and together they help you to achieve self-actualization.

Shift Your Paradigm

Dr. John H. Sklare said, "Thought reframing is the conscious and mindful act of taking some difficult, upsetting, or frustrating situation, thought, or emotional state and changing the way you look at it. Since your thoughts are what create your emotional states, changing your thoughts will change those emotional states. It's a conscious method of manipulating your thoughts as a way of changing how you feel. In laymen's terms, I guess you could say it provides a way to look for the silver lining that lies just beneath the surface of every dark cloud."[3]

Reframing is essential to managing your emotions and getting unstuck, because it helps you neutralize the emotional edge and filter information more effectively. The Reframing Model below is designed to help you to work through the reframing process by first focusing on yourself and your emotions and then extending your consideration to other stakeholders.

REFRAMING CONSIDERATIONS	
INTERNAL	**EXTERNAL**
Understand Your Emotions ►Identify your emotions and the thoughts Associated with them. ►Are you being overly negative or stubborn about something you can release? ►How can you reframe negative thoughts associated with your emotions?	**Understand Your Stakeholders** ►Who are the stakeholders and how are they affected? ►What are the opportunities for them? ►What are the risks? ►What are the power dynamics? ►What do you need to do the same/differently in relation
Identify Opportunities for Your: ► Development ► Empowerment ► Career/Personal goals ► Future Leverage ► Networking ► Transformation	**Recreate Your External Strategy/Plan** ►How do you reframe the thoughts behind a less than optimal strategy/response? ►What should you focus on? ►Do you need to change your typical response in any way? ►Why or why not? ►If so, what do you need to do to transform this into an opportunity? ►What is the right timing?

Table 11.1: Reframing Considerations.
Source: © 2011 Organizational Soul, Ltd.

The Reframing Considerations model provides an introspective tool to help you align your decision making with objectivity.

The internal quadrants take you through the steps of emotional literacy and emotional pattern recognition so you can get unstuck. Once you bring your emotions into your awareness, then you can choose to override or neutralize your emotions by reframing the situation.

After you work through the internal quadrants, you can move to the external quadrants, which are designed to focus you on analyzing situations externally. These quadrants are designed to help you think outside of yourself and create a constructive, holistic, emotionally intelligent response. The primary objective of the model is to help you approach reframing from both internal and external perspectives so you can create an integrative solution.

CASE STUDY #13: Randy's Poor Grade

Randy was a junior in college who received a grade of "C" for an assignment. The grade was much lower than he had expected. He was disappointed and angry because he had put extra effort into the assignment, so he set up an appointment to meet with his professor. In the meeting, Randy could choose to focus on the grade and argue each comment in an effort to persuade the professor to change his grade, or he could reframe the situation and view it as an opportunity to learn how to hand in better quality assignments in future.

If Randy reframes the situation and places higher value on learning, his professor can help him gain a deeper grasp of the subject or give tips about how to improve the quality of future submissions. This approach would help Randy to mitigate the risks of being blindsided by another unwanted low grade, his professor forming a negative bias toward him, and developing a superficial understanding of the material.

---

1 "Breaking Free from Self-Limiting Habits," at the Sword of the Spirit Ministries website by Innocent Mwangi, accessed December 2009, http://www.ssmk.net/breakfree.htm.

2 Nathaniel Branden, *The Power of Self Esteem: An Inspiring Look at our Most Important Psychological Resource*, (Florida; Health Communications Inc., 1992) pg 82.

3 "Change Your Thinking, Change Your Life," a 2006 article by Dr. John H. Sklare, on the Lifescript, Healthy Living for Women website, accessed December 2009, http://www.lifescript.com/Soul/Self/Motivation/Change_Your_Thinking_Change_Your_Life.aspx.

CHAPTER 12

ENCOUNTERING EMOTIONS SOCIALLY

Ongoing stress creates an energetic environment, affecting town and country, spreading from nation to nation, causing disharmony, disease, storms, and wars. The heart's intelligence can help to dissipate these negative stressful energies, giving people a fresh start in learning how to get along and live stress-free. As enough people learn about emotional fitness, it will cause a global shift into new consciousness that many are talking about and then quality of life has a chance of becoming better for the whole.

—Doc Childre

I N our work environments, we come into contact with numerous situations that can impact our quality of life and emotional stability. Based on my interactions with clients, here are some of the frequently encountered emotional systems that both trigger and represent emotive responses:

1. Jealousy and envy
2. Blame
3. Voicelessness
4. Self-Protectionism
5 Quiet Desperation

1. Jealousy and Envy

In various interviews with employers and employees, jealousy and envy is a divisive theme. One person described a situation where she was being left out of the communication loop so that information critical to her performance was being withheld by her manager. There was another person who described a situation where he felt unfairly treated because of hearsay, and because of this he verbally attacked his reporting officer. The decision maker never even bothered to find out the facts; instead, the decision maker accepted the statements at face value.

There are numerous ways that jealousy presents itself, and when it infiltrates any environment, it impedes teamwork and productivity because working relationships are impaired and trust levels are low to nonexistent.

Here is a list of situations that can attract jealous or envious responses:

1. When someone achieves something you wanted to achieve
2. When someone you dislike succeeds
3. When someone gets something you don't think they deserve
4. When someone seems to be favored by a decision maker

Jealousy in any situation is undesirable and destructive, but the intensity of jealousy tends to vary depending on how the jealous person feels about the target of his/her jealousy. At times, jealousy is open and detectable, and the target knows that they are not liked. Conversely, there are the undercover forms of jealousy that you cannot prove, and they tend to be more damaging.

Here are a three examples:

1. People planting seeds of doubt about you and twisting the facts without your knowledge.
2. People surreptitiously bad-mouthing your accomplishments or not acknowledging them. They intend to defame your character, performance, or skills so they can appear to be better than you.
3. Sabotaging behavior designed to put you in an unflattering light.

Sources of Jealousy

There can be many reasons why anyone can be jealous of you. Sometimes jealousy is centered on financial status; other times it is based on physical traits or style. For some, academic achievements can spark it; for others, it is lifestyle and possessions.

Jealousy is the result of a person's view of himself or herself. It surfaces when someone perceives you as having something she doesn't, and because she sees the world in terms of lack and not abundance, this makes her angry. Some jealous people will fake friendship and overextend themselves. Others will not even attempt to be congenial, because their mission is to openly bully you.

> **jealousy:** an emotion that typically refers to the negative thoughts and feelings of insecurity, fear, and anxiety over the anticipated loss of either something that a person values or a perceived advantage.

Fear also causes jealousy. For instance, when new, skilled people start working in a department, the fear of the unknown change in team dynamics causes jealousy, because there is the risk that the new people will drive up the standard of performance. This is frightening to the keepers of the status quo. People who are targets of jealousy can be discredited, sabotaged, and left out of communication loops. Other members of the team are sometimes forced to take the side of the jealous teammates, because they don't want the hateful behavior to be directed at them.

In their April 2010 *Harvard Business Review* article entitled, "Envy at Work," authors Tanya Menon and Leigh Thompson asserted that "envy damages relationships, disrupts teams, and undermines organizational performance. Most of all, it harms the one who feels it. When you're obsessed with someone else's success, your self-respect suffers, and you may neglect or even sabotage your own performance and possibly your career. Envy is difficult to manage, in part because it's hard to admit that we harbor such a socially unacceptable emotion. Our discomfort causes us to conceal and deny our feelings, and that makes things worse. Repressed envy inevitably resurfaces, stronger than ever."[1]

> **envy:** the desire to possess the same advantage that one witnesses in another individual or party.

Menon and Thompson also pointed out two side effects of envy: disparagement and distancing. People tend to disparage, either through minimization or exaggeration, to diminish the person who achieved something extraordinary, or they disparage the extraordinary outcome. This can lead to distancing or division within a team, and ultimately, it can cause weakened communication.

If You Are the Target of Jealousy

The root cause of jealousy is low self-esteem, so there is virtually nothing you can do to change the jealous people around you. Self-esteem building and empowerment are personal responsibilities, so attempts to help the jealous person can backfire.

Here are nine things you can do when faced with jealousy:

1. Be selective with the information you share about yourself. It can be distorted by malicious intent.
2. Refuse to lower yourself to the same level as the jealous people around you.
3. Know that you have a right to choose healthy relationships and healthy work environments.
4. Jealousy can sometimes present itself as bullying, so make a choice if you must.
5. Many people dumb down to minimize jealous attacks. This negatively affects you, your professional growth, and your ability to enjoy your job, because you are playing small. Be who you are; jealous onlookers will see your light no matter what you do.
6. Don't be seduced by friendliness. Robert Green, author of *The 48 Laws of Power*, stated that one of the laws of power is to "pose as a friend and work as a spy."[2] Beware of this type of jealous person. They can deceive you into misplacing your trust.
7. Another one of the laws of power is, "Do not build fortresses to protect or isolate yourself—isolation is dangerous." By falling into the isolation trap, you will not be able to build relationships, and consequently, you can become an easy target.
8. Build your emotional intelligence competencies.
9. Affirm yourself and what you do well. Understand that no one has exactly the same abilities, so focus on what you do well, and become the best at that.

Team leaders can help to minimize jealousy and envy by focusing on the strengths of members of the team and recognizing members for diversity instead of homogeneity. Menon and Thompson also suggested that team leaders can make scarce resources accessible and plentiful, so there is no competition for resources. They can share the power among members of the team, structuring team member roles so that no one feels disadvantaged.[3]

If You Feel Jealous

If you are typically negatively affected by other people's perceived success, understand that you are experiencing emotions somewhere on the spectrum of fear and anger. Once you identify your emotions, identify what your emotions are teaching you. Ask yourself why you are jealous or why you feel threatened by another person's talents or achievements. Then seek your talents; you have unique abilities, so cultivate your strengths by focusing on your goals.

When you identify the personal belief systems that are causing you to feel jealous, take conscious steps to improve in the areas you feel are underdeveloped. If this doesn't work for you, focus on your strengths. Learn to see yourself as empowered, and choose to reframe your thoughts so that you can perceive your personal potential clearly. We all have different talents and proclivities, so focus on becoming the best at what you do, and understand that everyone is different.

2. Blame

I always marvel when I sit in meetings when assigned actions were not taken, and the irresponsible manager would say, "I gave that project to one of my supervisors, and he was unable to get it done." The underlying message in this blaming statement is that the manager delegated the responsibility, so he doesn't have to be held accountable. Blame is typically an attempt to displace accountability and cover up your short-comings.

When you blame others for your shortcomings, you are appointing fault or responsibility to someone else in an effort to divert attention from your responsibility. This approach can slow down the decision-making process in some companies as the issue degenerates and becomes a matter of who is at fault instead of identifying what went wrong and how it can be fixed.

The members of a team all play a part in unmet goals. If you are a leader, it may be as simple as seeing someone struggling and not offering assistance, because it is her job, or it may be that you feel your instructions were clear. Whatever the reason, blame is based on your perception of the facts, and people who become agile blamers usually overuse the art of spin.

Blame can be intended as a criticism and is driven by emotions. It is really a form of cowardice, a lack of courage to admit to your mistakes. It sometimes happens in the presence of the person being blamed. In such cases, the person being blamed may not feel she is in a position to contradict the blamer because of the blamer's influence or position. This is just as cowardly as blaming someone in his or her absence.

Forms of Blame

Finger pointing: This is a straightforward form of blame. It is about using your perception of the situation to formulate a way to displace fault.

"You" Language: When you use "You" language, you point out how someone else contributed to the situation, overlooking your involvement. It takes you out of the equation altogether and is perceived as an attack.

Excuses: Many people come up with rational, compelling excuses and expect accountability to be waived. The bottom line is that the project or assignment should be done, and an authentic discussion should occur if you were unable to do something. Take ownership and make a commitment to correct the situation.

Planting the seeds of doubt: Some people have a system of blame they develop over time by planting seeds of doubt about someone else. This is done when a person questions someone else's competencies or relentlessly points out her shortcomings.

People using these tactics do this both in the presence of and behind the backs of their co-workers.

The Root Causes of Blame

Blame usually occurs when there is fear and distrust. In an office environment, when accountabilities and responsibilities are not clearly defined in job descriptions, there can be misunderstandings caused by responsibility overlap. As a leader, one of the first steps in ensuring you create the ground-work for an environment of professionalism and collaboration is to prepare job descriptions.

Blame is a self-preservation tactic. It is used to cover up perceived incompe-tence when there is fear of embarrassment or personal attack. Some of us prefer to deflect rather than suffer humiliation. Another reason why blame occurs as a self-preservation tactic is because some people may read any form of criticism, constructive or otherwise, as an attack. Rather than suffer through a perceived attack, they prefer to deflect responsibility.

Another reason people may blame others is because they link performance to their earning potential. They don't want their salary increase or bonus to be affected by anything or anyone, so they protect their earning potential by blaming others. Always keep in mind that making yourself look good by making others appear incompetent is not a sound tactic. It can catch up with you and expose you.

There are people who assign their self-worth to being perfect. They fear any perceived form of failure and associate failure, no matter how small, with repu-tational risk. They don't realize that blaming sacrifices their reputation.

The Aftermath of Blame

Blame is a destroyer of trust. At its root is fear, a lack of integrity, and a lack of emotional discipline. Here is how blame can affect your team:

1. Reduced productivity.
2. Reciprocal doubt. When doubt is created, it has a way of being reflected back at the person who created the doubt, because distrust moves like a virus.
3. The real team issues may remain undefined and unattended to, because they are buried beneath the blame game.

No one can win the blame game. If you are a blamer, it may appear that you have won, but you are whittling away the trust of the team.

Creating a Blame-Free Environment

Take appropriate responsibility. There are people who take responsibility for more issues than they should, and there are others who take responsibility for nothing. If you are assigned a project, whether you delegated the project or parts of it, you are responsible until the goals are met. Ask what part you played in the creation of this situation or what you could have done differently.

Build your Integrity: Admit when you are wrong, say what you intend to do to correct the situation, and then correct it. If you are a leader, remember not to blame your team; they are an extension of you.

Avoid taking sides: In many instances, multiple parties have contributed to the situation.

Seek the Facts: If you can extrapolate the facts and focus on a solution, you can get things done. Otherwise, you will get mired in unproductive discussions about who is at fault. Use discernment to understand the real issues, and then set the objective to take a fair course of action.

Use emotional intelligence to change your blaming behavior by:

- Identifying your emotional patterns: Do you feel destabilized when something goes wrong? Is blaming someone else an optimal solution for you and the team? Once you identify your emotions and patterns, take responsibility for the circumstances. Fear usually drives blaming behavior. Identify your fears and take concrete steps to overcome them.
- Thinking about the consequences of your actions. As a leader or member of a team, you should always be aware of the possible outcomes of your actions or inactions. If you can master this skill and think about possible consequences of your actions and make corrections, you can proactively prevent problematic outcomes.
- As a leader, manage blaming discussions by focusing the group on the facts and not taking sides. Also, remember to recognize your biases or assumptions. Blamers will always come to you with spin and will draw you into their web if you allow them.

Protect Yourself from Blame

You can't stop anyone from blaming you for anything, but you can nullify the effects of blame by establishing authentic relationships with your co-workers and reporting officer.

Transparence: One way to protect yourself from blame is to let your reporting officer know what you are doing. We tend to feel we shouldn't have to "blow our own horns," but keeping your reporting officer in the loop (within reason) can protect you. Be sure your reporting officer and co-workers have provable facts so other people's opinions can't compromise your efforts. This means you need to communicate effectively. Keep in mind that some of the right people to communicate with need not include your reporting officer. There may be people of influence at lower ranks within the organization that management and your co-workers listen to and trust.

Maintain your integrity: Be someone your reporting officer can trust so that if you say something, you will be believed and respected, especially when things go wrong and your co-workers are actively pointing their fingers at you.

3. Voicelessness

When we are recruited into a company early on in our careers, we believe in ideals. We expect everyone to work together and anticipate environments that are safe spaces where employees can speak up and contribute safely. New employees can easily fall into this trap. Your reporting officer asks for your thoughts on a subject during a meeting. You were lulled into thinking the question is authentic so you state your true position in the meeting, but your ideas are not what the reporting officer wanted to hear. Not only are you attacked with overt ferocity at the meeting, but also you are attacked every time you state your ideas in a meeting. Your manager either wants to be sure you will agree with everything or not say anything. From this manager's viewpoint, saying nothing is fine, because she doesn't want disagreement that can potentially expose her knowledge or competence gaps.

Other employees fight their reporting officer to the point where they end up being terminated, which also suits the reporting officers, because they are sending a clear message to the employees who remain: "Don't you dare! If you go against me, your job is not safe."

This cycle of behavior reminds me of a pirate T-shirt I saw that said, "The beatings will continue until morale improves" with a picture of a skull and crossbones underneath. I thought this was an excellent metaphor for what sometimes happens in the workplace. Although we don't use physical whips, we do use words, behaviors and the emotions behind them as whips.

Verbal attacks create a false sense of harmony that unaware managers read as high morale. Morale appears to be at a satisfactory level, because the attacked people are reluctant to admit there is a problem. They know the reporting officer can make life exceedingly difficult at work either through constant attacks or by ignoring them completely, so they are selective about what they say.

There are team members who know something is wrong—perhaps a process was incorrectly completed or someone was unfairly accused—but they won't speak up, because speaking up implicates them in the mistake in some way, and they do not want to be linked to the error.

Employees aren't the only ones hesitant about speaking up. Some managers are afraid to speak up for their staff to their reporting officers. These managers don't have a voice in the organization, so they can't effectively represent their employees.

Other managers are ill-equipped to handle confrontational or abusive employees, so they avoid these employees, allowing inappropriate, hostile behaviors to infiltrate the team. Abusive employees really need direction or corrective action, and by ignoring them, the reporting officer weakens the entire team.

Some managers appear to allow opinions but manipulate the discussion back to their way of thinking. Employees see manipulation for what it is, and it can have the same impact as a frontal attack because in the end, people will not contribute when the effort is viewed as futile.

There are managers who always speak about an "open door" policy—they even leave their doors open—but employees rarely enter their office, because they usually encounter an unwelcoming attitude. Either the manager is busy typing while the employee is speaking, or the manager constantly takes calls. Others are abrupt or short with employees.

Some reporting officers avoid employees who want to have a voice, because the reporting officer has something to hide, or because they can't handle the truth. It may be that the reporting officer is being confronted by an unfair decision, or the reporting officer may just not like the employee and wants him to suffer. They don't understand or care that if you negatively affect one person on a team, the entire team is impacted.

Speaking up is about having a voice in your company. Some companies are disciplined about inviting employees to contribute and state their cases, because they value creativity, conflict management, and team building. These management teams consistently invite dialogue, take corrective action when appropriate, reward innovative ideas, and support their staff in developing their creativity.

In other work environments, speaking up is viewed as uninvited. The managers want everyone to sing from the same song sheet, not understanding the power of harnessing diverse views and integrating those views into a stronger solution.

When managers give employees the latitude to express themselves, the manager should ensure employees are equipped with ground rules and skills to help them to express themselves constructively. This helps everyone feel valued and helps the organization to grow.

The ability to speak up is a function of the emotional competence and openness of the leadership team. They are the primary architects of the culture of a company, so here are a few ideas for leaders who are ready to create a safe environment that sets the stage for employees to contribute their ideas and thoughts:

1. Dialogue with executives

Some employers recognize that not listening to employees will lead to low morale and cause the management team to make the wrong decisions or miss opportunities for innovation. With this in mind, some companies arrange meetings where groups of employees dialogue with the president or another executive who will listen to employees' suggestions and challenges and take action.

2. Seek alternate forms of communication

There are companies that encourage employees to make suggestions using other communication tools. They use company blogs, employee hotlines, employee surveys, or an intranet to accept and respond to feedback. These tools are usually backed up with a process for reviewing suggestions and comments, taking action, and communicating the actions or decisions to employees. University of Texas assistant professor of management, Ethan Burris, stated in an article called "Missing Voices: Why Employees are Afraid to Speak Up at Work" that "Formal transparent follow-up is very important. It is counterproductive to ask an employee for feedback if you never do anything with that information. If staff see their ideas just disappear, they'll stop offering them all together."[4]

Some employers develop leaders who use emotional intelligence when communicating so they can navigate their emotions and biases. They want to be sure that managers are responding to ideas and not external personalities or internal emotions.

To facilitate the transition to speaking up, some employers train employees to help them communicate more effectively by supporting their ideas clearly while demonstrating respect.

Speaking up is really about opening top down, bottom up, and lateral communication channels. Sharing important information, listening to employees, and implementing their ideas helps them feel valued and connected to the organization.

4. Self-Protectionism

In his book, *Biology of Belief*, author Bruce Lipton points out that if cells exist in a safe, nurturing environment they grow and evolve. Alternatively, when cells are in a perceivably dangerous environment, they shift into a protective mode where they either attack or withdraw.

Dr. Edgar Schein, a professor at the M.I.T. Sloan School of Management and a pioneer in the theory of organizational culture, asserts organizational culture is created through observable and acceptable behaviors, group norms or standards, rules of the game (politics), habits of thinking, and generally accepted symbols of status. The architects of organizational culture are not limited to the owners and executive team, but the primary responsibility for developing a culture lies with them. In fact, Schein asserted that organizational culture doesn't usually survive in its current state if the primary culture carriers separate from the organization.[5]

There are four typical organizational cultures: predominantly controlling, competitive, collaborative, and creative. Controlling, political, or competitive environments can become so toxic that employees who would normally share their ideas in a collaborative work environment withhold their input, because they are concerned their ideas will be rejected or attacked unceremoniously. An obvious result of political and controlled cultures is that they can stifle creativity, lower risk-taking proclivities, and perpetuate self-protectionism.

Typically, collaborative, and creative environments are nurturing and safe. Employees in these cultures are usually engaged, continuously growing, and sometimes even have fun. These types of workplaces reduce the need for self-protectionism and increase risk-taking tendencies and synergy.

Recognize if you are in a Protectionist Mode

There are people who spend time determining which career they want, but don't put the same effort into evaluating work cultures that are compatible with their personalities, values, and needs. As a result, these people can end up doing something they love in an environment that stifles their growth.

In toxic organizations where pettiness and counterproductive actions of the team leaders perpetuate the need for self-protectionism, growth is very difficult. If you are in a self-protection mode and would like to move to an open, nurtured growth mode, here is how you can transition:

1. Determine whether you are in the right job.
2. If the work environment you are in is not be the best for you, you can either decide to stay, or you can create an exit plan designed to transition you to another department or company.
3. As Mahatma Gandhi once said, "We must be the change we wish to see in the world." You can only change yourself, and if you are not one of the primary drivers of the culture then decide if you are in the right work environment for your stability and progress.
4. Avoid becoming something you are not. Do not allow an environment to influence who you are and how you interact with others. Always see yourself as empowered to exercise choice, even though your salary may be supporting your desired lifestyle.

Transform your Environment

If you are a leader or business owner and are one of the architects of the culture of your organization, here are six tips for transitioning your culture to one that supports a platform for safety, openness, and transformation:

1. Be aware of the behaviors you exhibit and reward. You should emulate the changes you would like to witness within your staff.
2. Understand changes will sometimes be necessary within your leadership team. Key people who are perpetuating the old culture may have to be replaced by people who can hold the culture accountable to the new and desired standards.
3. Leaders will not only have to demonstrate new behaviors, they will need to be consistent. For instance, if a culture is one where team leaders humiliate employees for unwanted contributions, they will need to demonstrate consistent coaching behaviors that invite an open and safe developmental environment. Employees will not trust the change at first, so consistency is not negotiable.

In addition to consistency and role modeling, leadership characteristics of being confident, action-oriented, and charismatic can support the transformative process. These behaviors support buy-in, engagement, and trust.

Edgar Schein suggested that during the cultural change process, leaders should be aware of what they pay attention to, how they react to critical incidents, how they achieve results, how they allocate scarce resources, and the criteria they use to reward employees.[6] Awareness of these behaviors can help them to embed desired cultural norms.

In the midst of any cultural change process, your team needs to learn how to adopt the change, avoiding a superficial approach where the new behaviors are superimposed on the old paradigm and merely cover up the perpetuation of old behaviors. Clarity, transparency, accountability, and effective communication plans are essential. As the change process takes place, chaos will happen before the dust settles. It becomes clear how power will be redistributed, what the new cultural boundaries are, and which behaviors will be rewarded.

5. Quiet Desperation

When I speak to employees, a majority of them feel a sense of entrapment. They need a job, especially during difficult economic times, but they feel underutilized and helpless about finding the work that brings them joy or excitement. They feel invisible and unable or unwilling to do anything about it. Others feel overtly victimized.

I hear many stories, but one particular example stands out. There was a supervisor named Joe who was asked to meet with his team to share information about a change in his department. He was reluctant to schedule a meeting, because whenever he held a meeting, his manager reacted negatively if she was not invited, and attacked the staff if she was invited.

Inviting her would not be a challenge if employees were comfortable being authentic in her presence. So on one hand, Joe should hold meetings but would rather not experience the mental and emotional anguish of being raked over the coals. Therefore, Joe avoids meetings at all costs. As a result, there is stagnation, poorly informed employees, a lack of trust, and a huge need to preserve self within his department.

There aren't enough leaders who take interest in mentoring, so some talented employees end up stuck doing the same thing repeatedly. As a result, employees are not stretched. Instead, they are left to their own devices to develop themselves.

Career stagnation may occur when less talented but more political, spin-savvy co-workers continuously attempt to show up other employees, using their relationships with executives and powerbrokers to manipulate information about you and anyone else they view as a competitor. They may not be as competent as you, but they are blessed with the gift of gab and can talk their way into the jobs they desire.

Powerlessness is a state of mind. When you think you are powerless, your mind is playing a trick on you, causing you to believe that you are forced to accept your situation. Some scholars link it to pessimism because pessimists view circumstances as though they do not have a choice.

You Have a Choice

The first step in digging yourself out of your perceived predicament is to realize that you always have a choice. You have a choice about which company you work for, your department, whether you move to a new job, and if you decide to move, when the best timing is. When I meet people who believe there is no choice, most times I find they have not developed a blueprint for their career or personal development.

I have viewed many career development plans. Some employees plan to move up the hierarchy within the company, and others are open to moving within an industry. There are employees who are not interested in a promotion, because they don't want anyone reporting to them or are about to retire. Other employees are preparing to change career paths or even open their own company. There are even business owners who feel trapped by their business. They become tired of the routine and start to resent having people who are dependent on them for a salary.

Always recognize that you have a choice. Resist buying into the deception that you have no alternatives. If you get creative, no matter your age or educational background, you can find something you can do.

There is also the question of risk. Should you risk making the decision? If so, how will it impact you and your family? Should you jeopardize your future?

When you think you don't have a choice and you remain immobilized, you are making a choice to go with the flow. Why not put yourself in the driver's seat? When you start perceiving your options, you feel less trapped, more alive, and less affected by apparent stagnation or immobility.

---

1 Tanya Menon and Leigh Thompson, "Envy at Work," in *Harvard Business Review*, April 2010.

2 Robert Green, *The 48 Laws of Power*, (New York; Penguin Books, 2000), p.101.

3 Tanya Menon and Leigh Thompson, "Envy at Work," in *Harvard Business Review, April 2010*, p. 5.

4 Burris, Ethan, "Missing Voices: Why Employees are Afraid to Speak Up at Work," in *University of Texas, The McCombs School of Business Magazine*, Spring/Summer 2009.

5 Schein, Edgar. (2001). "Organizational Culture and Leadership." *Classics of Organization Theory*. Jay Shafritz and J. Steven Ott, eds. 2001. (Fort Worth: Harcourt College Publishers).

6 Schein, Edgar. (2001). "Organizational Culture and Leadership." *Classics of Organization Theory*. Jay Shafritz and J. Steven Ott, eds. 2001. (Fort Worth: Harcourt College Publishers).

CHAPTER 13

EMOTIONALLY COMPETENT COMMUNICATION

To effectively communicate, we must realize that we are all different in the way we perceive the world and use this understanding as a guide to our communication with others.

—Tony Robbins

E FFECTIVE communication is an art that requires self-discipline, critical thinking, emotional intelligence, curiosity, and openness to perceive and interpret other people's perspectives. The intensity of your emotion and your underlying needs can influence your motive to communicate effectively, so it is important to understand what is driving your needs to effectively manage yourself.

Maslow's Hierarchy of Needs: A Communication Application

In Chapter 11, we discussed Maslow's Hierarchy of Needs in the context of getting unstuck. Now we will evaluate Maslow's model from the perspective of emotionally competent communication. When you view communication through the lens of Maslow's Hierarchy of Needs, you are observing communication from various levels of the hierarchy. For instance, when a manager is communicating with an employee about the many errors the employee is making, the manager may be communicating from a need level of safety and security, because the employee's performance directly affects the manager's performance. The employee may respond from the same level of need or from a different level such as belonging.

Depending on the emotional intelligence and self-awareness skill levels of the manager and employee, the communication can play out where the manager is communicating in autocratic, parent mode, so the employee adopts a resistant, child mode. This type of exchange will inevitably lead to anger and frustration for both parties. Alternatively, the same manager may communicate with another employee who rarely makes errors in an adult mode, discussing ideas and solutions. This conversation may sound more self-actualized and less emotional, because it is based on respect and openness to diverse points of view.

Maslow's Hierarchy of Needs

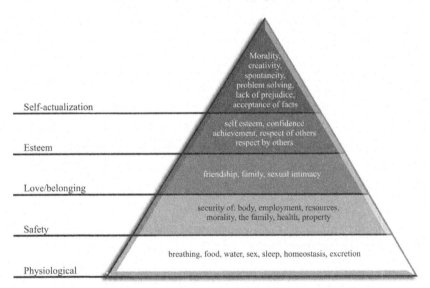

Figure 13.1: Maslow's Hierarchy of Needs
Maslow, Abraham, "A Theory of Human Motivation" Psychological Review #50(1943) p370-396, American Psychological Association, adapted with permission.

Figure 13.1 identifies the levels of Maslow's Hierarchy of Needs so that we can explore how they relate to effective communication.

Physiological Needs: People who are concerned about meeting their physiological needs are preoccupied with physical concerns, such as hunger, fatigue, or pain. Communication attempts in this state can be pointless or difficult until the physiological need is satisfied. For instance, if a student is hungry, it is very difficult for her to concentrate on her schoolwork or a lecture. In this case, hunger is an overriding experience and acts as a barrier to communication until the hunger is no longer an issue.

Safety and Security: Some of us communicate from a place of needing to feel safe or secure, so we choose tactful words and ideas that do not rock the boat. Alternatively, there are circumstances where reserving your comments may undermine your safety and security. One reason is that inaction can be misinterpreted as agreement or taking a side, and you can lose valuable resources or opportunities because of inaction.

For example, in highly political environments there are employees who are preoccupied with not rocking the boat, because they want to maintain some semblance of safety within their work environment. An accumulation of unspoken thoughts can lead to misunderstandings, because communicators formulate unchallenged assumptions, decisions, and assertions. This type of unidirectional system of communication can be toxic and may lead to unnecessary misunderstandings or low morale because feelings of voicelessness cripple the majority.

Love/Belonging: People who communicate from a place of belonging are secure, and someone meets their intimacy needs. There are different types of intimacy, but we will focus here on emotional intimacy. Dr. Brenda Shoshanna writes, "True emotional intimacy begins with willingness to be who you are— to express yourself honestly and fully and to know that your partner is able to accept you as you are. This also includes the reverse—your being able to really listen, understand and accept your partner and what he needs to share."[1]

As we can see emotional intimacy creates a strong bond. If this type of intimacy shifts unexpectedly from one person to another, relationships can be damaged, because the shift changes the dynamics of the first relationship, creating a void. If the person in the first relationship is attuned to the relationship, the change lowers the level of trust, and over time, creates suspicions that can lead to emotions such as betrayal and anger. If the person in the first relationship has a high need for belonging combined with low self-esteem, he can become a target for manipulation, because safety and security become a priority at any price.

Self-Esteem: Self-respect and respecting others is central to communicating with self-esteem and managing both your emotions and the tone of the conversation. Author Karl Perera tied self-esteem and confidence together when he asserted that "self- esteem increases your confidence. If you have confidence, you will respect yourself and then you can respect others, improve your relationships, and choose happiness. This is not a selfish goal as you will contribute more and share yourself with the world and those around you. Low esteem can lead to depression, unhappiness, insecurity, and low confidence. Other desires may take preference over yours. Inner criticism, that nagging voice of disapproval inside you, causes you to stumble at every challenge and challenges seem impossible."[2]

From an emotional intelligence perspective, self-esteem directly relates to your ability to view the world from a place of optimism and empowerment. Pessimists communicate from a place of low self-esteem, because they have an inherent philosophy of "I can't."

Self-Actualization: CEO & author Bo Bennett asserts, "Those who improve with age embrace the power of personal growth and personal achievement and begin to replace youth with wisdom, innocence with understanding, and lack of purpose with self-actualization."[3]

Different theorists view self-actualization from different perspectives. Kurt Goldstein likens self-actualization to the force or drive to find your purpose. Abraham Maslow described it as "the desire for self-fulfillment, namely the tendency for him [the individual] to become actualised in what he is potentially."[4] Maslow identified the self-actualized as fact-focused, spontaneous problem-solvers who are not judgmental.

The two theories converge where qualities of autonomy, independence, intrinsic motivation, and an ability to transcend the environment intersect. From another vantage point, self-actualized people can be highly skilled at all emotional intelligence competencies. They have a strong capacity to navigate their emotions and communicate effectively.

Communication Dynamics

David Berlo's communication model (Figure 13.2) is comprised of four components: source, message, channel, and receiver. The basic theory is that messages originate from a source who encodes a message for a channel to a receiver. To explore the connection between Berlo's model of communication and emotional intelligence, let us consider an emotional communication loop. For example, an angry client is being rude to a customer service representative. The message is encoded by the client with anger both verbally and non-verbally and the customer service representative, who is on the receiving end of the emotive message, can make the choice to decode the message without thinking about the consequences of his actions or he can navigate his emotions and respond to the client professionally. By listening and applying emotional intelligence skills like empathy or realistic optimism he can terminate the negative emotional virus.

There are people who attempt to master verbal communication at the expense of their mastery of nonverbal communication. The result is that your emotions come through despite your choice of the right words. In cases where emotions come through your message either verbally or nonverbally, there is the potential for increased emotional escalation for both the sender and receiver.

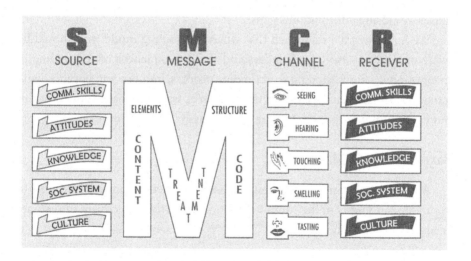

Figure 13.2: Berlo's Model of Communication.
From BERLO D. *Process of Communication*, 1E. © 1960 Wadsworth, a part of Cengage Learning, Inc. Reproduced by permission. www.cengage.com/permissions.

The Communication Loop: Encoding

The person speaking encodes a message for the listener at both verbal and nonverbal levels. Effective verbal messages are clear in meaning, aligned with nonverbal language, and free from jargon. The sender's culture, values, emotions, communication skills, and knowledge formulate and filter verbal messages. Once the message is transmitted from the sender to the receiver, the receiver's sensory channels process the messages first.

The Communication Loop: Decoding

Once the communicated information is filtered through the listener's experiences, biases, training, emotions, and other perception-forming receptors, a unique meaning is assigned to the information. This can trigger a regulated response, but it can also trigger a premature irrational response. The listener needs clarification before an emotion is adopted and expressed.

As the receiver of a message, if you have refined, active listening, self-management, and articulation skills, you will be in a position to decode the message transmitted by the sender. Paraphrasing, reframing, critical thinking, and questioning for understanding help the listener to understand facts or root causes by closing informational gaps.

We have already established that when in listening mode, you should be aware of your emotions and understand the consequences of responding in an emotional state. Listening is a complex process, because you have to distill spoken and unspoken messages of the speaker as well as manage your emotions and your natural propensity to tune in and out every few minutes.

Barriers to Listening

A number of barriers can compromise the listening process and lead to misunderstandings. For the communication loop to flow effectively, the listener needs to overcome these barriers:

1. *Emotions*: Worry, fear, anger, grief, stress, depression, excitement, joy, and exuberance all impede the listening process.
2. *Individual biases and prejudices*: From Berlo's perspective, biases form part of our encoding and decoding filters in the area of your values. Cultural experiences developed by family and religion drive your values. Your biases can reinforce miscommunication, so they need to be uncovered and challenged.
3. *Preoccupation with your point*: Sometimes we are so preoccupied with

our point of view because of our biases, that we are unable to perceive another perspective. Unrelenting behavior of this type can lead to the listener feeling disrespected, because the speaker is not allowing the listener to have a voice. This sets the stage for emotional escalation.

4. *Boredom*: When you are bored, you tend to tune out because the information is of no interest to you. This can lead to feelings of disrespect and emotional escalation.

5. *Short attention spans*: Some people have short attention spans, so, depending on the topic, your communication style and other internal and environmental factors, they may tune you out completely.

6. *Thinking ahead of the speaker*: Sometimes we think ahead of the speaker, assuming we know what they are going to say. This can deconstruct the communication process because the speaker forms biases about the listener. Possible biases include perceptions that the listener is disrespectful, arrogant, or mentally challenged.

7. *Physiological Problems*: These problems are distracting and lead to more tuning out because of a physical state. Tuning out is only one possible effect. If there is pain, there is probably stress, and stress can lead to abrupt, caustic, or impatient remarks.

8. *Environmental Noise*: Some people are skilled at tuning out environmental noise while others are very distracted by it. We all have differing thresholds with background and foreground noise, and a display of emotion can emerge if the ability to concentrate becomes a challenge.

Nonverbal Communication

Mastering your nonverbal language requires developing an awareness of your body language and your associative, unconscious, nonverbal language patterns.

Tips for Improving Your Communication Skills

- *Maintain eye contact.* Shifting your eyes away frequently from the speaker may indicate that you are not listening or that you have something to hide. Maintaining eye contact provides the speaker with information about you and gives you information about the speaker, because the contact serves as a connection. Eye contact helps you with listening, because it adds information to the message from the sender while concurrently providing the speaker with information.

- *Give open, nonverbal responses while the other person is talking.* While you may not agree with what they are saying, you want the speaker to feel free to state her position. This is especially useful when attempting to build an environment where people feel safe to speak up.
- *Don't let your nonverbal language reveal your emotional state prematurely.* Body language speaks volumes because it is a strong indicator of your authentic emotion. As a result, untrained or undisciplined body language can be a better predictor of what you are thinking than your verbal expression of your thoughts. People tend to react to the emotions coming through your body language, so it is important to align your nonverbal communication with what you are saying or learn to manage them better.
- *Remain alert during lengthy conversations.* Take notes if you find it necessary to manage your attention span. Always remember, it is impossible to not communicate. Saying nothing says something.
- *Avoid behavior that can be perceived as an attack.* Name-calling, shouting, and profanity can all be perceived as an attack and cause an escalation in emotion.

When Communication Is Not Received As Intended

Many people have value structures that compel them to tell the truth no matter what. While truth-telling is viewed as a respectable trait, some people have not developed the emotional competence to determine when telling the truth is crossing the line into the realm of abuse. Here are a few considerations to help you to develop optimal truth-telling strategies:

- *Timing:* Mastering the art of timing is useful when you decide to tell the truth. This may involve determining the people to tell first, or it may require delaying the information release to the right time, because emotions are in a heightened state. Mastering the art of timing is important for strengthening your credibility and helps you to avoid labels such as loose cannon or complainer.
- *Honesty and Disclosure:* Understand the difference between honesty

and disclosure and determine whether or when disclosure is appropriate. When I suggest this difference, I am not recommending that you lie by omission. Here is an example to support the distinction: a mother has two children and she secretly favors one of her children. Mothers generally don't intentionally disclose this information to any of their children because although it may be true, disclosure in this case is destructive, unnecessary, and inappropriate.

> **honesty:** fairness, truth, and straightforwardness in conduct with others. Not disposed to cheat or defraud; not deceptive or fraudulent.
>
> **disclosure:** the act of making a previously hidden revelation evident.

- *Understand How People React to You:* If you are a team leader, understand how people react to you. Do you tend to find out about errors team members make long after the fact? Does it seem that members of your team are hiding things from you? Perhaps they are doing so because they find your honest approach blunt, humiliating, or dehumanizing.
- *Summon Curiosity:* When appropriate, find a way to communicate the truth from a place of curiosity, non-judgment, and support instead of from blame, judgment, or bias. The truth can be communicated in a respectful way and leave the person to whom you are speaking with their dignity. It is important to keep in mind that there are times when a blunt approach is necessary, because some people only respond to this type of communication.

Communicating with emotional competence is a daily journey. Some days will be easier than others, because emotions change as your relationships go through their normal fluctuations.

Self-regulation through emotional management can help improve the quality of your communication. Keep consequential thinking in the forefront of your verbal and nonverbal exchanges so that you are contemplating the consequences of your words and actions and minimizing the need for damage control.

---

1 "Four Steps to Becoming Closer (Developing Emotional Intimacy)," an article by Dr. Brenda Shoshanna at the SelfGrowth website, accessed December 2009, http://www.selfgrowth.com/articles/Four_Steps_To_Becoming_Closer_Developing_Emotional_Intimacy.html.

2 " Self Esteem is the Key to Your Happiness and Well Being," Home page at More-Self Esteem, a website by Karl Perera, accessed December 2009, http://www.more-selfesteem.com/self_esteem.htm.

3 Bo Bennett, *Year to Success*, (Massachusetts; Archieboy Holdings, LLC, 2004).

4 Abraham Maslow, "A Theory of Human Motivation," A. H. Maslow (1943), Originally Published in *Psychological Review* 50, (1943) p. 370–396.

CHAPTER 14

USING EMOTIONAL INTELLIGENCE TO NAVIGATE CONFLICT

The direct use of force is such a poor solution to any problem; it is generally employed only by small children and large nations.

—David Friedman

EMOTIONAL intelligence is one of the essential tools for short-circuiting conflict. It can help you identify sources of latent conflict and provide the tools you need to navigate conflict as it emerges, focusing you and others involved on solutions. Emotional intelligence can also facilitate your ability to explore other points of view and work toward outcomes that may not be popular but are designed to de-escalate the conflict.

Conflict Resolution Modes, Transactional Analysis, and Emotional Intelligence

The Thomas-Kilmann model[1] defines five modes of conflict resolution. Like any tool, the five conflict resolution styles can be applied appropriately or inappropriately. To avoid inappropriate, automatic responses to conflict, you can develop mastery of conflict resolution styles, combined with the ability to operate from an adult ego state with emotional intelligence.

Before exploring conflict resolution styles, I would like to investigate the Transactional Analysis theory, which plays an active role in conflict stimulation, escalation and resolution. Eric Berne, the father of the Transactional Analysis theory, authored a book called *Transactional Analysis in Psychotherapy*.[2] He contended that people communicate from the ego state of a parent, adult, or child. Depending on which ego states are interacting, conflict can arise.

> **conflict resolution:** the ability to resolve conflicts between disagreeing parties in an effective manner.

According to Berne, in the parent state, a person can interact with others from a place of control or nurturing. A controlling parent may be bossy, critical, and faultfinding. Nurturing parents are balanced or may teeter into the domain of suffocation and over-indulgence. In a child-ego state, you might be compliant, curious, resistant, rebellious, anxious, or immature. Overly-critical and overly-indulgent parent types communicating with someone from a rebellious or immature, child state can provoke conflict. On the other hand, when two people are communicating from an adult-ego state, they can be cooperative, playful, or nurturing. From an emotional intelligence perspective, adult communication is rational and self-regulated.

Integrating the Thomas-Kilmann Model of Conflict Resolution with Emotional Intelligence

In reality, conflict is a necessary part of our existence. When managed skillfully, starting with self-regulation and then focusing on the big picture, it can be a creative process instead of a destructive one. Conflict can start under the surface of relationships, and when something triggers a reaction, it emerges. Confrontation can become intractable when there is a lack of emotional competence and other negotiation skills on both sides. If the parties to the conflict are able to get past a stalemate and de-escalate the situation, they will have to rebuild relationships, because neglecting to rebuild trust sets the stage for another intractable situation.

The Thomas-Kilmann model of conflict resolution suggests five basic styles of conflict resolution that differ in combinations of assertion and cooperation. Using emotional intelligence, you can apply the right resolution style or combination of styles to drive a constructive process and outcome, harnessing the conflict.

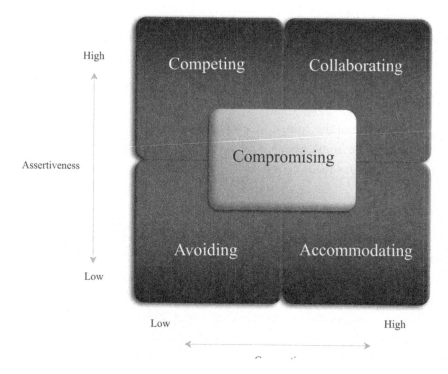

Figure 14.1: Emotional Intelligence Applications of the
Thomas-Kilmann Model of Conflict Resolution
Source: *Thomas-Kilmann Conflict Mode Instrument*— also known as the
TKI (Mountain View, CA: CPP, Inc., 1974—2009)

Conflict Resolution Styles

Conflict resolution styles can be effective if you are able to manage your emotions and focus on the facts instead of the prevailing personalities. With conflict, it is optimal if all parties can self- regulate, but in reality, you only have control of yourself. All the styles represented by the Thomas-Kilmann model have appropriate and improper applications. Your ability and willingness to use all the styles will provide you with a strong arsenal when you encounter conflict.

The Competing Style

People who use the competitive conflict resolution style prefer a conflict approach that is highly assertive and very low on cooperation. Parent-to-child communication can fall within this category and so can adult-to-adult communication.

Behavioral Pattern

People who use the competitive style rely on power or force to get what they want. While some people will avoid or accommodate this approach, others may take an equally competitive stance and arouse conflict.

Strategic Implementation

There are times when the competitive conflict resolution style is strategically correct. For instance, a unilateral decision can be acceptable if there is insufficient time to collaborate. This style is also strategically correct if relationship maintenance is not a priority or when an unpopular decision is made. This style always presents the possibility of an aftermath characterized by resentment or bruised egos, so it is wise to understand the consequences of this approach before taking action.

The Collaborative Style

The collaborative style is high on the scales of assertiveness and cooperation. When all the participants in conflict are collaborating from an adult state, you have a good shot at reconciliation. If there is a shift into parent or child modes, the quality of communication can plummet to a less than optimal level.

Collaboration can be time consuming, so it requires the availability of time to be effective. It is also important to note that collaboration without decision-making can be ineffective, so there may be a time where collaboration has to be transmuted into a competitive style so a decision can be made.

Behavioral Pattern

Collaboration occurs when people provide their points of view with the goal of solving a conflict. The aim of this style is to integrate different perspectives into a solution, so everyone should be heard.

Strategic Implementation

Collaboration is a useful tool when you need to integrate different views, there was conflict in the group previously, and you cannot afford to make a trade-off to resolve the issue.

The Compromising Style

Medium levels of assertion complemented by medium levels of cooperation characterize compromise. It involves giving up something to get something in return. A person in a parent ego state may compromise with a rebellious person in a child state, or a person in a child state may compromise with a belligerent parent.

Behavioral Pattern

Compromise involves some level of sacrifice that can lead to eventual gain. Choosing compromise as a solution requires the use of consequential analysis, so you can perceive the short-, medium-, and long-term costs and benefits of your actions. Compromise also requires the ability to navigate your emotions, so you aren't stuck in a spiraling emotional state that can cause you to overlook compromise as an appropriate option or to rely on it too heavily.

Strategic Implementation

Compromise is used as a tool of negotiation. If you do not have an attachment to an outcome, you may decide to concede to a demand so you can leverage the gesture in a future negotiation. This is a purely political motive designed to build a power base.

Compromise is also a useful tool if there is a fast-approaching deadline or if the conflict is at an impasse, because it is a complex problem with no clear solution. It is also applied when the costs related to prolonged negotiation processes outweigh the benefits.

The Avoiding Style

People who implement an avoiding style are low on assertiveness and low on cooperation. While sometimes this is a healthy strategy or response, there are times when it is a fear-based strategy that is deployed when there is a bully or other type of difficult situation.

Behavioral Pattern

When fear is driving an unconscious avoidance response, you may be taking a risk. You risk avoiding an issue that requires a different response. For instance, bullies can view avoidance as weakness, and as a result, they can persist with their behaviors. One pattern feeds the other pattern, creating an uneven power distribution.

Strategic Implementation

If your avoidance pattern is purely based on fear, it would be useful for you to explore your fears so you can mobilize yourself. For others, avoidance is a deliberate tactic used because the costs of taking action outweigh the benefits. In such cases the avoider may view the issue as trivial or doesn't want to react to the symptoms of a deeper issue.

The Accommodating Style

The accommodating conflict resolution mode is low on assertiveness and high on cooperation. Depending on the person, accommodation can occur even when surrendering your position is not necessary. From an emotional intelligence perspective, this type of accommodation suggests the person may be extrinsically motivated, sacrificing internal needs for external reward. For example, some people accommodate because they do not want to be bullied or humiliated if they have a different point of view.

Behavioral Pattern

In some cases, the accommodation style can indicate low self-esteem, because low assertiveness is often associated with low self-esteem. Some people describe accommodators as being "pushovers." While this may be true in some cases, low assertiveness can also show up as a decision made by someone with very healthy esteem.

Strategic Implementation

Accommodation is used if the outcome means more to the other party than to you. As with compromise, accommodation can be used as political tool for future leverage. Others accommodate when peace is more important than winning. It is also important to note that accommodation can be a beneficial resolution style when one of the parties to a conflict wants to minimize her losses.

Conflict-Driven Environments

There are different conflict-driven environments, and the difference between them is the skill and will of the leadership team. In some environments, leaders harness conflict into a constructive, innovative, and creative process. Leaders in this type of environment value the growth and development of the team and are skilled at knowing how to ensure the environment doesn't move to extreme, ruthless behaviors.

These leaders are vigilant about maintaining a constructive environment by promoting and rewarding collaboration, creating synergies, encouraging healthy debate, and demonstrating intolerance for signs of emergent toxicity. These leaders recognize the signs of latent conflict and are unafraid of the prospect of harnessing differences. Some companies are very serious about protecting their cultures, and if a new hire is not the right fit, they will not hesitate to terminate the new employee despite his technical competencies and experience. They find ways to constructively manage each situation, because leadership in an environment characterized by conflict is both an art and a science.

Other work environments are highly political and dominated by unhealthy tension and destructive conflict. Cutthroat antics, character assassination, harassment, and disrespect are only some of the traits leadership teams employ in a highly political environment. This breeds similar behaviors in all staff.

In overly political environments, attempts at leadership through modeling constructive conflict resolution behaviors are typically met with venomous reactions if there is not enough of a critical mass of skill and will for building a positive environment. Highly political environments flourish on undermining behaviors, and although it is possible to effect change, some leaders do it at a price of self-sacrifice, because they position themselves for character assassination, constant harassment, or attack.

Navigating Different, Difficult People

We often label people who are different from us as difficult. These differences create the illusion of conflict because of our inability to manage our thoughts and emotions effectively. Moving toward personal and professional effectiveness in diverse or difficult environments requires the development of your emotional competence.

Developing your emotional intelligence is usually a work in progress, because years of automatic response patterns are hardwired by our thought associations. When this happens, it is particularly difficult to remain rational when someone says or does something that pushes your hot button.

Let us explore the different people who can arouse emotions within you and create conflict if your emotions remain unregulated. We will also investigate what you can do to respond in an appropriate manner, keeping in mind that appropriate behavior may require assertiveness.

Types of difficult people

- Hostile people
- Complainers
- Jealous people
- Critics
- "Stressed-out" people
- Drama attractor
- Unresponsive people
- Liars
- Fundamentalists
- Bullies

Hostile People

These people are generally not in listening mode. They are entrenched in their opinion and intent on confronting you, which makes it difficult for you to reason with them. Depending on the situation, there are times when you can diffuse their anger by listening and empathizing. Other times, you can wait until they cool off, because if you make an inappropriate response, the situation may become irreversible and unbearable.

When you are interacting with a hostile person and applying emotional intelligence, one advantage is that you know exactly what you are experiencing and how you can navigate those emotions. If you perceive the hostile situation as one that is transforming over time, use your emotional intelligence tools of pattern recognition, consequential analysis, intrinsic motivation, and realistic optimism to help you to transform hostile, competitive situations into more productive exchanges. Supplemental tools of using the right timing, listening, empathy, curiosity, and interest-based discussions are strong complements to your emotional intelligence.

From a conflict resolution perspective, hostile behavior is highly competitive. There are times when an equally competitive response may be necessary or vital, because someone makes an unpopular decision. You can rely on your emotional competence to manage through the change, diffuse emotional responses, and help another adapt.

Complainers

Complainers are interesting because they always seem to have a black cloud of negativity hovering over them. They operate from a base of victimhood, complaining about their frustrations from a place of powerlessness. The paradox with complainers is that some organizational or familial cultures do not allow them to have a voice, because they are labeled as chronic negativists whether or not they have valid or even brilliant points. Their voicelessness occurs because no one wants to hear another complaint; they want to hear about solutions or alternatives. In some cases, leaders just want absolute, mindless compliance.

Complaining is high on the assertiveness scale and low on the cooperation scale, so it is viewed as a competitive response. If you tend to complain, it is important to manage your emotions and choose the optimal conflict resolution style. For instance, by providing alternatives, you can shift to a collaborative mode. By choosing your battles, you can shift to an avoiding mode. Mastering the competencies of communication, timing, optimism, and consequential thinking can help you to break the label of complainer.

Jealous People

Jealousy can cause stasis in any environment and is usually the result of low self-esteem, because it rears its head when you view yourself as being or having less than others. It may be that you do not travel in privileged social circles or that you do not demonstrate qualities or skills that are rewarded or recognized in the workplace or at home.

Model of Critical Feedback

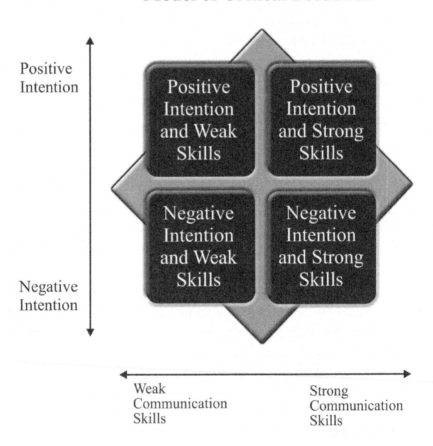

Figure 14.2: Model of Critical Feedback
Source: © 2011, Organizational Soul, Ltd.

Jealousy arises as a result of extrinsic motivation driving the need to have what others have, ignoring your exceptional qualities. One way you can transmute this destructive mode of thinking is to establish personal goals and a plan to achieve them. Another way may be to seek professional help designed to build your self-esteem and help you understand there is no need for you to compare yourself to others, because everyone is equipped with unique assortments of talents and abilities.

The presence of jealousy at work can cause withdrawal or inhibition. Inhibition can arise because some people who are capable of contributing to improved results would rather not be the target of jealous behaviors, so they dumb down, back off, or take conscious steps to remain invisible. Sometimes jealousy emerges when leaders attempt to create healthy competition because their lack of perception and skill create undesired dynamics.

Jealousy can also show up if members of a group detect favoritism, because a leader unconsciously created a system of reward and recognition that excludes most people. Some leaders tend to reward traits that are similar to theirs, because diversity makes them uncomfortable.

Critics

From the perspectives of intention and communication skill, there are four types of critics:

Figure 14.2 illustrates four types of critics based on the dimensions of their intention and communication skills. When people criticize with positive intentions and weak communication skills, they can be the catalyst for just as much conflict as critics with negative intentions and weak communication skills.

Critics with good intentions and underdeveloped communication skills may come across as judgmental or caustic. They mean well but can leave a destructive trail of withdrawn people who prefer not to engage the critic, because they are tired of constant judgments.

Alternatively, critics with good intentions and underdeveloped communication skills may be so tactful that the true message is lost.

Critics with negative intentions and strong communication skills may take a little longer to leave a trail of destruction, because their emotional intelligence and other interpersonal skills may initially camouflage their negative intentions. Others may leave a deliberate trail of destruction by using their communication skills to trigger negative responses.

Constructive critics with developed communication skills possess the rare ability of expressing their opinions without being condescending or judgmental. They are open and inclusive, and their communication style is inviting. Constructive critics recognize they are not perfect, so they use their emotional competencies to identify when their communication is approaching a destructive tone. If this happens, they can recalibrate by demonstrating curiosity and heart as opposed to impatience, boundaries, and bias.

Critics with negative intentions and weak communication skills can exhibit corrosive, antagonistic behaviors that are carefully designed to instigate destructive conflict. Others may deliberately withhold critical information. Whether the behaviors are aggressive or passive-aggressive, negative intentions can generate damaging emotional responses and low morale if not managed effectively.

Stressed-Out People

High stress levels can lead to an impaired ability to manage your emotions. When you are stressed and something compounds your stress, you may not be in the frame of mind to navigate your emotions. One of the true tests of your emotional intelligence is what you do when you are under pressure, so stressful situations are an opportunity for you to become more deliberate or conscious about choosing the higher, emotionally competent road.

From a conflict resolution standpoint, unbridled stress can lead to inappropriately avoiding issues because self-preservation or safety and physiological needs are at an overwhelming level. In cases like this, building relationships through critical thinking, self-navigation, and conflict resolution artistry are impossible. Unbridled stress can also lead to wanton demonstrations of emotion, so in such cases, you can become the catalyst for conflict. In other situations, your lack of self-regulation due to high stress levels can cause you to sustain or feed existing conflict.

Reducing stress can help to facilitate the de-escalation of conflict. Reducing stress may mean you decide your environment is not the right one for you, so you quit your job or take on less responsibility. As a student, it may mean you chose the wrong major, so you decide to make a change no matter what your parents think. From a personal perspective, you may decide to confront a stressful home situation so that you can manage yourself and bring E.Q.

Librium to your personal environment. Reducing stress can also mean taking a much-needed break to focus on yourself, seek insights, and create plans. Taking a break can help you get into a "flow state" that can help you to tap into your circumstances at a much deeper level.

Drama Attractor

If you are a drama attractor, you have constant commotion in your life. You hardly ever see yourself as a contributor to the perpetual state of drama around you, so you assign responsibility to everyone else. Understandably, the drama persists because you have created the illusion of victimhood. The first step in resolving this toxic pattern is to realize that you are an active participant in your reality, and you can seek to change the patterns of behavior that are attracting or creating unnecessary drama and destabilizing you.

Drama creators exist in an unconscious world where they are blindsided by other people's responses because they are blissfully unaware of their drama producing behaviors. One type of drama producer is the person who has to fight to make a point. She thrives on a highly combative process and enjoys the thrill of the fight. She wants to win at any cost, creating consequences, because relationships cannot survive the continuous onslaught of fighting.

The Unresponsive Ones

If you are unresponsive, either you say nothing and let others do all the talking, or you talk in circles, never adding value, repeating yourself in different ways, creating an endless communication loop. Another type of unresponsiveness is answering questions with questions. Whichever tactic you choose, your lack of a direct reply can lead to frustration, suspicion, and ultimately a lack of trust.

Another type of unresponsive behavior is being overly agreeable. This is an avoidance strategy, and it reduces team effectiveness, because overly agreeable behavior can translate into favor-seeking behavior. It is perceived as artificial. No one, including team leaders, trusts yes-people, because constant agreement reduces team effectiveness, increases the political level, and impedes constructive conflict.

In some situations, people eventually ignore unresponsive counterparts, because people who make overtures to include you are not usually successful at deepening relationships with you. If you are a co-worker or manager working with an unresponsive person, all you can do is create space where it is safe to speak up and share opinions. You can use communication tools, such as curiosity, acceptance, constructive advice, and recognition to draw out the unresponsive person.

From a conflict resolution perspective, unresponsiveness is perceived in a number of different ways. It can be viewed as a passive-aggressive tactic that is high on the assertiveness scale and low on cooperation. On the other side of the spectrum, it can be perceived as an avoidance strategy that is low on assertiveness and cooperation.

Liar, Liar

If you tend to rely on giving untruthful accounts to make it through your day, you are probably in a highly political work environment. Overly political environments are rife with people who tell creative untruths. They use distortion tactics, such as minimization, distraction, blaming, or exaggeration that can lead to misunderstandings, false senses of security, missed deadlines, inaccurate reporting, or inferior results. These tactics undermine healthy team-building activity by impeding trust.

Alternatively, there are leaders who believe that trust undergirds enhanced results, because it creates safe space for employees to be vulnerable enough to make mistakes and learn from them. Trust allows constructive criticism, enhanced working relationships, and creativity so that fairness can prevail. From an emotional intelligence standpoint, lies create consequences whether or not the truth is exposed. Decisions are made based on lies, relationships are destroyed because of lies, and execution plans are based on untruthful assertions. It is important to note that emotional intelligence and integrity can be mutually exclusive. Emotionally intelligent people are capable of telling lies and wreaking havoc, using their emotional competence to enhance their story, its delivery, and acceptance.

From a conflict resolution perspective, lies are often used to avoid situations, take a competitive stance, collaborate, compromise, or accommodate. It is important to keep in mind that lying undermines the conflict process, because it creates the potential for escalation each time a lie is revealed. It will also impede the trust-building process during the post-conflict, peacekeeping phase.

Fundamentalists

Fundamentalists tend to interpret information aligned with their belief systems as literal, because of an established internal code of adherence. When in a fundamentalist mode, lateral or critical-thinking skills are not easily accessible, despite the capacity for it, and emotion can emerge if a personal belief system is challenged in any way.

If you embark on a journey to change the opinions of a friend or co-worker in a fundamentalist mode, you may be stoking the fires of emotion, relentlessness, and destructive conflict. Remember that it is highly unlikely that you will nullify or reverse long-held biases that are deeply embedded in a person's belief configuration, so try to avoid destabilizing yourself and others emotionally by attempting to change someone else's beliefs.

Some managers are embodiments of policies and procedures. They take a fundamentalist approach to organizational policies, missing the true intention of the policies and getting trapped in a cycle of literal application. While there is a place for policies and literal application, there are circumstances that are not an exact fit and fall outside the ambit of documented policies. In cases of ambiguity, the spirit of the policy needs to be understood and used as a guideline, but not everyone is capable of operating in the realm of ambiguity.

Some fundamentalists choose to avoid conflict by agreeing to disagree or by not addressing differences. Avoidance can feed latent conflict, so while it provides short-term relief, it can lead to extended conflict. If people with fundamental views can use collaboration effectively, they are equipped to integrate multiple points of view. Unfortunately, collaboration is not always possible with fundamentalists.

Bullies

Bullying encompasses people who are vindictive, jealous, micromanagers, hostile, duplicitous, or relentless with their attacks. Sometimes it may seem almost impossible to please a bully, even when you think you are doing what the bully wants you to do.

Bullies lurk around offices and feel they can create an air of superiority when they devalue members of their team. They don't welcome new ideas; in fact, innovation threatens some bullies so much that they reject an idea as not viable, claim to have already thought of it, or criticize both you and the idea.

If an employee threatens a bully manager, a number of tactics can surface. Some bully managers insist on having employees follow instructions to the letter. They don't allow thinkers to think. They want blind obedience, which can lead to employees not having a voice. Some manager bullies are uncomfortable with intelligent employees who are straightforward and capable of stating their true opinions. While freethinking employees are unafraid of speaking their minds initially, bullies perceive freethinkers as a risk, so the bully's survival instincts activate, with you in their cross hairs.

Workplace bullies harass co-workers in different ways. They make veiled or overt threats or withhold or conceal something you earned. Some manager or supervisor bullies take control to extremes by constantly keeping tabs on employees, calling them frequently during work hours and personal time. Their verbal and written communication reeks of disrespect, pettiness, and the need for control.

Unpredictable bullies fluctuate emotionally from being easygoing and friendly to angry, vindictive monsters who spew insults and caustic criticisms without discrimination. The psychologists may call it a bipolar disorder. Everyone else views this behavior as a nightmare. These environments can be palpable with the tangible fear of the next surprise attack.

There are no limits to the tactics bullies employ. They can negate everything you say, tell lies, take unfair disciplinary action, or frustrate you with unneeded assignments and impossible deadlines. Bullies ignore or interrupt you, sabotage you, display negative body language, or hurl angry insults at you.

Employees feel trapped by a bully because if they tell the bully about the undesirable behavior, the bullying will almost certainly worsen. If employees report the behavior to a lawyer, they could experience other complications that jeopardize their jobs. From the perspective of Maslow's Hierarchy of Needs, people subjected to bullying are sometimes operating from a lower level need for safety and security, and despite the need level, performance can result. However, even though people can perform under duress, enhanced performance can result if members of a team can coexist respectfully in an environment.

Where there are bullies, there is fear or tension. Everyone on the team feels it, no matter who is the target. When this happens, employees tend to move into avoidance mode, because they don't want to be faced with any type of direct assault resulting as a consequence of confronting the behavior.

If your attempt to resolve a bullying situation through your business or organizational leaders does not work, your leaders either don't believe the allegations are serious, or they approached the bully inappropriately. Others allow bureaucracy to get in the way of an effective solution. There are business owners or senior executives who are afraid or compromised and cannot take definitive action against the bully.

Bullying can surface in any type of relationship: professors bully students, students bully one another, parents bully their children, customers bully service providers, co-workers bully one another—the possibilities are endless.

The Costs of Bullies

Bullies can create opportunity costs within an organization, because interaction with them is avoided unless direct interface is necessary. An overused form of accommodation is telling the bully what he wants to hear. If accommodation is the chosen path of the majority, your results or objectives are compromised, new or important ideas are suppressed, employee or member morale is low, the quality of customer service suffers, and you can lose good employees to the competition.

How to Navigate a Bullying Situation

Bullies can be stuck in their behavioral patterns because they don't view themselves the way others perceive them. If the bully in your life has a higher social status than you have and may affect your career or personal life, you need to decide if this situation is an optimal one for you. You can only change yourself, so talking to the bully about how you feel is rarely effective. Here are a few more tips:

- Identify your options. Unfortunately, if you are being bullied you may think you are trapped, so you may not resist the disrespectful behavior. By identifying your options, you can identify alternative courses of action for yourself that will allow you to break out of the cycle of bullying. Sample courses of action could include handing in your resignation after finding a new job or career, escalating the situation to your union representative, or requesting a transfer. It is important that you convert from a pessimistic, powerless approach to an optimistic approach that focuses you on opportunities or alternatives.

- Some bullies seek you out relentlessly, so if you can, limit the access of the bully.
- If you have assessed the situation and it makes sense, fight and win the right battles. Fighting a bully is a competitive process, because the bully wants to win by overpowering you. Choose your battles wisely, because bullying is a persistent phenomenon, and fighting may cause you to end up being a martyr.
- Yield when appropriate. Constantly fighting with a bully is pointless if the actions or avoidance of decision makers support the bully. In fact, constant retaliation can have an adverse effect on your career.

Emotionally Intelligent Conflict-Resolution Tools

Your ability to tap into and use emotionally competent strategies in the face of conflict implies that you have a tool kit you can utilize to help make the conflict-resolution process more palatable. Self-regulation in the face of conflict involves:

Self-Knowledge

- Managing yourself
- Managing your thoughts
- Defining your personal values and priorities

Self-Regulation

- Displaying optimism
- Tapping into intrinsic motivation
- Forgiving
- Knowing when to quit

Engaging Others

- Managing your environment
- Adopting a big-picture perspective
- Diffusing emotions

Self-Knowledge

Managing Yourself

The first step in managing conflict is to manage your internal world. This means you need to understand the emotions and patterns that surface when conflict presents itself in various forms. For example, do you tend to become assertive or even aggressive in the face of conflict? Or do you choose to stick your head in the sand or accommodate?

Managing Your Thoughts

Author Wayne Dyer states, "Your behavior is based upon your feelings, which are based on your thoughts."[3] However, there is physiological evidence that this process is not necessarily a linear one, because in situations characterized by high anxiety, emotion can precede thought. No matter what comes first, thought or emotion, thought management is critical to self-management.

Once you can manage your thoughts and emotions, depending on the situation, you may choose to remain calm or respond with an appropriate emotion. If you choose to respond with emotion, it will be a conscious decision, not because of a reflexive action. If you choose to remain calm, active listening skills can help you to diffuse an emotionally charged situation.

Define Your Personal Values and Priorities

Your relationships, emotions, family traditions, beliefs and values create the filters you use to interpret situations. For example, your reporting officer may give you and another co-worker a project to collaborate on, and you know the project result is important to the team. You are new to the team and you want to impress your reporting officer, so you want to show him that you can finish the project quickly and accurately. Unfortunately, you are paired with a co-worker who is disillusioned by the company, because he has been overlooked for a promotion for five years. Your co-worker is not motivated and does not demonstrate an iota of interest in the deadline. In this example, each employee has developed different emotional filters, and consequently, their approaches to the project are dissimilar and incompatible.

There are times when you have to rearrange the prioritization of your value system so you can change your emotional response both internally and externally. For example, I had a conversation with an executive who was placing more emphasis on the value of getting the work done than on leading and inspiring. He got the work done by being blunt, abrupt, and impatient, and his results were pretty good, but he was exhausted by his constant frustration. The team was demotivated and silenced by what they perceived as inhumane treatment.

After employees complained about the executive's communication style to the CEO, the executive received training and coaching and eventually balanced his priority values in a way that included results, developing people, and exercising patience through self-management. Even though the results of the team were already satisfactory, his change in focus and behaviors led the team to higher performance and improved morale. He was still focused on getting the work done, but the values of developing others and treating employees with respect increased in importance, transforming the situation.

Self-Regulation

Optimism

Practicing optimism is another useful way to navigating conflict. Optimism exposes possibilities. As we established, as an optimist you do not see yourself as powerless or helpless; you know you always have choices and that conflict resolution is creative process that may take time.

I can recall an employee, Rhonda, who stopped talking to her co-worker, Penny, because of something Penny allegedly said about Rhonda. Rhonda was sworn to secrecy, so she was not able to tell Penny there was a problem, but she became increasingly uncomfortable with Penny so she avoided her. Penny noticed the change in Rhonda's behavior and could not understand what was wrong, so over time, trust eroded for her as well.

One day, the supervisors chose Rhonda and Penny to collaborate on a project, so they now had to communicate. Given the lack of trust, their communication was limited, tentative, and political. Neither Rhonda nor Penny was willing to address the trust issue, so the conflict remained latent.

Intrinsic Motivation

Your ability to balance your intrinsic thoughts, needs, and drive with extrinsic pressures is important. Your intrinsic motivation is a function of your self-esteem, and your ability to guide yourself internally despite external pressures. It helps you remain focused on your goals and your system of values.

Forgiveness

Stanford Professor Frederick Luskin stated, "My research also shows that as people learn to forgive, they become more hopeful, optimistic, and compassionate. They become more forgiving in general."[4] Forgiveness is a very useful tool. It is about letting go of perceived injustices and deciding to take the high road. Forgiving does not mean you should be a pushover and give in; it means is that you should learn to yield.

Some people think forgiveness is about reconciling with the perceived transgressor. A close friend of mine sums forgiveness up as loving from a distance. He means that he is at peace with the situation and is cordial with the perceived wrongdoer but will not allow the person into his inner circle again. Luskin further defines forgiveness saying, "Forgiveness and justice are not the same. Forgiveness and reconciliation are not the same. Forgiveness and condoning are not the same."[5]

Knowing When to Quit When Faced with Conflict

Another competence you can use in navigating conflict is knowing when to quit. Some people hold onto their opinions stubbornly without thinking about how they can collaborate. The following considerations should be taken into account when deciding when to quit:

1. Understanding the price you will pay if you continue to hold onto your point.
2. Seeing the situation from a big-picture perspective.
3. Understanding the right timing. If you do not think about all the

contributing factors to the conflict, you may take too long to quit and jeopardize important relationships. Alternatively, you may quit too soon and undermine your leverage and credibility.

4. Understanding the players and what motivates them.
5. Identifying your values and their priority. If you are holding onto something that is a low priority, you may be putting yourself at a disadvantage and putting your team at risk over something that is not a priority.

Knowing when to quit entails weighing the facts so you can determine when to give someone another chance or when to stop giving them chances altogether. There are times when we give people so many chances that we undermine our own effectiveness, and become known as pushovers. Making a decision to quit requires balancing emotions and facts to make an effective decision.

For leaders, knowing when to quit is about knowing when to separate from a member of your team versus giving him another chance. There are team leaders who wait without thinking through the skill gaps and creating a development plan for the employee. This undermines the leader's credibility.

Knowing when to quit also involves knowing when to persevere. Sometimes perseverance is the right strategy in the short- and long- terms. At other times, yielding in the short-term can allow you to persevere in the long-term.

Engaging Others

Managing Your Environment

Once you can manage your emotions, you can use your skills to help manage the emotions within your environment. Here is a list of tips you can use to contribute to managing your environment successfully:

- View the situation from a big-picture perspective
- Help diffuse the emotions of others
- Consciously apply conflict management strategies

View the Situation from a Big-Picture Perspective

The Irish Dramatist, Oscar Wilde, wrote, "We are all in the gutter, but some of us are looking at the stars."[6] Transforming your vantage point when viewing an emotional situation will help you to perceive the whole picture. This is essential to creating an effective approach to managing conflict.

Big-picture thinking enables you to perceive multiple perspectives and synthesize the information in a simplified form. Author Andrew Sobel provides a few tips about what you can do to develop your big-picture thinking skills. Here are a few of his suggestions:

- Develop multiple perspectives
- Look for patterns and commonalities
- Understand relationships between events (history)[7]

I would like to add two points to Sobel's list:

- Understand relationships between people. People are an integral part of most decisions even though we may focus on the process or content of the proposed change. Relationships between people can positively or negatively impact a decision, so the web of relationships (culture, internal politics etc.) needs to be a primary consideration when considering the big picture.
- Perceive the long-term impact of your decision. Big-picture thinking is often linked to making a decision, so fine-tuning your ability to deliberate the outcomes of alternative decisions will help you to make better decisions. This is because you are considering the processes and outcomes related to each alternative, so that you can find the best match between your final decision and your initial objectives.

It is interesting to note the same skills needed for perceiving the big picture are essential for enhancing your emotional intelligence.

Diffuse the Emotion of Others

Diffusing the emotions of others starts with listening intently when another person is emotional and speaking. The emotion can be joy or anger, excitement, or frustration. Whichever the case, the emotional speaker has a limited capacity for listening to you, so wait for the speaker to become grounded so that he or she can listen to your idea or point of view. Diffusing emotion also requires reserving your point of view and empathizing until emotions have dissipated. It is implied that right timing is a part of this process.

Consciously Apply Conflict Resolution Strategies

If you are in an emotional state and not thinking clearly, your conflict strategy should not be a short-term response that may be ineffective for getting you where you want to go in the end. Emotional responses range from a highly assertive automatic response or bring-it-on attitude that engages the conflict to an avoidance or accommodation mode because you just want the conflict to stop.

It would be helpful to consciously change your state from being closed to conflict to being more open or even curious, if you can achieve this. Transforming conflict from a destructive mode to a constructive one starts with understanding that no conflict is personal.

Conflict usually emanates from a person's impaired confidence, competence, or internal fears. When fears surface, a response can take a matter of seconds, especially when emotions are heightened. Another tool that can help with changing your approach to conflict is to reside in a place of acceptance. It means you should listen first and not let your assumptions and biases impede your critical thinking and the quality of your communication.

---

1 *Thomas-Kilmann Conflict Mode Instrument*— also known as the TKI (Mountain View, CA: CPP, Inc., 1974—2009)

2 Eric Berne, *Transactional Analysis in Psychotherapy*, (New York; Ballantine Books 1986).

3 Wayne Dyer, *You'll See It When You Believe It: The Way to Your Personal Transformation,* (New York; Harper Paperbacks; 1 edition 2001) p. 50.

4 Dr. Fredrick Luskin, *Forgive for Good: A Proven Prescription for Health and Happiness,* (New York; Harper One; 1st Edition, 2001)

5 *Ibid.*

6 Oscar Wilde, *Lady Windermere's Fan, 1892, Act III,* Play (1892)

7 Jagdish Seth and Andrew Sobel, *Clients for Life: How Great Professionals Develop Breakthrough Relationships,* (New York; Simon & Schuster; 1st edition 2000), pg. 151.

CHAPTER 15

OFFICE POLITICS

You know who is good at office politics, people with empathy, people who are great time managers, and people who see themselves as part of a team. Which means, of course, that you should get good at office politics, because the people who are bad at it have dead-end careers and spend their lives whining about how it's not fair because they are so good at doing their work.

—Penelope Trunk

THERE are leaders and employees who choose not to engage the political games people play at work, because they associate being political with lacking integrity. In other words, they are unable to perceive office politics from a place that is not judgmental, so they decide against participating in the political games and end up wondering why their careers have plateaued.

In *Survival of the Savvy*, Rick Brandon and Marty Seldman discuss three political styles: overly political, under-political, and savvy.[1]

Overly-Political People

They are preoccupied with form instead substance, prepared to do whatever it takes to win, care only about themselves, and lack integrity.

> **office politics:** the use of one's individual or assigned power within an employing organization for the purpose of obtaining advantages beyond one's legitimate authority. Those advantages may include access to tangible assets, or intangible benefits such as status or pseudo-authority that influences the behavior of others.

Overly-political players often get ahead despite the fact that they may not possess the skills needed to be successful in their current roles or in positions of high authority. They are perceived as go-getters and have a high opinion of themselves. These people thrive in person-centric environments where position, power, and hierarchy drive decisions and rewards.

> **force:** the use of tactics designed to give a person an advantage over an individual or group. It is coercive: to cause to do something through pressure or necessity, by physical, moral, or intellectual means.
>
> **authentic power:** power that is derived from an internal source of integrity. People who demonstrate authentic power take full responsibility for their experiences or emotions. Authentic power is connective because it is based in internal congruence and empathy. The demonstration of authentic power can lead to others demonstrating their own authentic power.

Force versus Authentic Power

Inauthentic and authentic power differ based on the intention behind the action(s). Inauthentic power can be a forceful, controlling, deceptive, or aggressive approach that does not consider the ideas of the person being coerced. Table 15.1 outlines commonly used inauthentic power tactics that can lead to dysfunctional responses based in anger or fear.

INAUTHENTIC POWER TACTICS	
Promising and not delivering	Bullying
Telling lies - This includes exaggeration, minimization, spin and flattery.	Allowing private agendas to overide the agenda of the team.
Passive aggression	Sabotage
Witholding information	Manipulation
Taking credit for someone else's work	Status seeking, name dropping
Blame	Refusal to admit mistakes

Table 15.1: Inauthentic Power Tactics.
Source: © 2011, Organizational Soul, Ltd.

AUTHENTIC POWER TRAITS	
Persuasive	Love
Emotional self-discipline	Inclusion
Integrity	Healthy detachment
Cooperation	Forgiveness
Trust	Internal harmony with values

Table 15.2: Authentic Power Tactics.
Source: © 2011, Organizational Soul, Ltd.

Authentic power comes from an internal source of integrity. It is inclusive and allows others to demonstrate authentic power. Table 15.2 describes the traits of persons who exhibit authentic power. Authentic power is linked to emotional intelligence because it takes emotional competence to set the stage for authentic power.

Gary Zukav said, "An authentically empowered person is incapable of making anyone or anything a target. An authentically empowered person is someone who is so strong or so empowered, that the idea of using force against another does not enter into his consciousness"[2]

Zukav made an important distinction between power and authentic power. In a book collaboration with Linda Francis, Zukav goes on to give advice about how you can balance inauthentic power. He said very simply, "A power struggle collapses when you withdraw your energy from it."[3] But this is often easier said than done.

Substance Focused People

Brandon and Seldman assert that the under-political person places emphasis on integrity, substance, open agendas, and high performance.[4] They judge people who sell themselves and their accomplishments, because they perceive this as self-aggrandizing behavior. Usually, under-political people are highly competent, and if they are in an idea-centric environment, they can flourish, because substance, transparency, and meritocracy prevail. If under-political people coexist in a people-centric, highly political environment, it will behoove them to either become politically competent or find an environment that is better aligned with their style of self-management. From an emotional competence perspective, under-political people in highly-political work environments are often frustrated, because they are surpassed by people with lower competence and stronger willingness to forego integrity to succeed.

Politically Savvy People

According to Brandon and Seldman, savvy people combine the best characteristics of the under-political and overly political types. The politically savvy value integrity highly, and they understand and accept the need to engage the political games. They engage the games people play based on a value system of integrity as a fundamental building block.[5] This means they will position themselves and their accomplishments, but will do so with integrity.

Publicizing accomplishments at work can be subtle or overt. Some people are more comfortable with this approach by setting up a metric reporting structure designed to provide their managers and executives with achievement related data. Others will just tell their reporting officers how good they are. Your approach should align with your values, beliefs, and priorities.

Position Based Power Structures

Overly-political people place emphasis on power structures by using relational manipulation, and force as sources of power.[6] You will encounter highly political people in any area of your life, so it is helpful to understand and then engage power structures based on your value system.

The perception of possessing power is based on the view that someone has more of something than you do. Table 15.3 illustrates examples of situations where power can be perceived based on inequitable distribution of resources:

Symbols of Inauthentic Power

Education	Race
Expertise	Gender
Bullying	Relationship/Network
Celebrity	Delegated Authority
Information	Organizational Position
Money/Wealth	Communication Skill

Table 15.3: Symbols of Inauthenic Power
Source: © 2011, Organizational Soul, Ltd.

When seeking to demonstrate the right behaviors, we tend to consider one side of diversity: how we can treat people with respect, regardless their backgrounds. In order to fully appreciate diversity, we need to understand the power dynamics created by a lack of diversity consciousness. Displays of one-upmanship, where one person perceives themselves as being in a privileged position, can create the illusion of power.

Applying the Thomas-Kilmann Conflict Model to Politics

Figure 15.1, the Thomas-Kilmann conflict model, can be used as a basis for the discussion of power, because power structures can be underlying drivers of conflict.

Emotional Intelligence Applications of the Thomas-Kilmann Model of Conflict Resolution

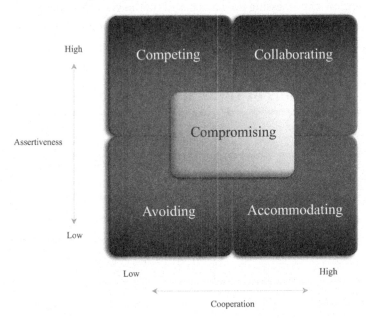

Figure 15.1: Emotional Intelligence Applications of the
Thomas-Kilmann Conflict Resolution.
Source: *Thomas-Kilmann Conflict Mode Instrument*— also known as the TKI
(Mountain View, CA: CPP, Inc., 1974—2009)

Competing in Political Environments

In a competitive political environment, people compete for a position of power and authority. An example of how power can be competitive is two political co-workers vying for the same job within an organization. They may choose tactics such as manipulation, gossip, or sabotage to get ahead of their competition.

From an emotional competence perspective, the competing style usually leads to a win–lose consequence, so before using this style, you will need to explore your openness to the possibility of losing. As with every style, sometimes it is politically savvy to be competitive, even if you lose, because you stood up for the right thing, at the right time, in the right way.

Collaboration Mode

Collaboration happens between people who are open to working together toward a mutual goal. In a collaborative environment, the power is equally distributed so two or more people can collaborate whether or not they have similar ideas. Before you decide to collaborate, be sure to understand the motives of the person with whom you are collaborating, because someone who is substance focused collaborating with someone who is very political may unwittingly end up in a competitive situation.

Compromise

Attempts at compromise can evolve into competitive or overly political behavior if it is not managed using emotional intelligence. Compromise can occur between any combinations of under-political, overly-political, or savvy people.

As previously indicated, compromise is a tool that can be used as leverage for future needs. The politically savvy and the overly political know and use this information, but the under-political may not be open to creating leverage, because they perceive this as a manipulation.

When used as a tool for leverage, compromise can be used with different motives. For example, the politically-savvy individual may be transparent and collaborate with you on how they will leverage the compromise. The overly political may hide their true motives and use the leverage as a tactic that serves their personal agenda. From an emotionally-intelligent perspective, the under-political types can use consequential thinking to consider using compromise as a tool from a base of integrity. When using compromise with integrity, under-political types are intrinsically motivated to use compromise to serve the agenda of the greater good.

Avoidance

The under-political prefer not to become entangled in overly political webs, so they tend to evade putting themselves in a position where they will have to engage in power plays. From an emotional intelligence perspective, avoidance can be driven by emotions of fear or caution. Short-term avoidance strategies implemented at work by under-political people sometimes are sometimes short sighted. One reason for this is that they may neglect to consider the possibility that people who avoid situations can be perceived as possessing deficient interpersonal skills. Unfortunately, this can cause career stagnation.

Savvy and overly-political people can also choose to avoid issues but for different reasons. Their reasons can be empowered or manipulative. For instance, savvy and overly-political people can choose to avoid a situation because it is not their problem, someone else can do a better job, they have nothing to gain, or they manipulated someone else into taking on the challenge.

Accommodating People

Accommodating behavior is highly supportive and lacks assertiveness. Savvy and overly-political people may choose to use accommodating behavior because they recognize they can use this approach as leverage. The under-political type tends to accommodate because they don't want to engage overly-political machinations.

The Spectrum of Political Styles

There are many types of responses and combinations of responses to highly and less political work cultures. Samuel, Bacharach, the McKelvey-Grant Professor of Labor Management and director of the Institute for Workplace Studies at Cornell University, defines political competence. He says, "It's the ability to understand what you can and cannot control, when to take action, who is going to resist your agenda, and whom you need on your side. It's about knowing how to map the political terrain and get others on your side, as well as lead coalitions."

Differences Between Political Styles

SUBSTANCE BASED APPROACH	POLITICALLY COMPETENT APPROACH (Integrity based)	SELF POSITIONING APPROACH
Acknowledging people's ideas as their own	Acknowledging people's ideas as their own	Stealing people's ideas
Keeping your achievements to yourself	Advising people of your performance	Blowing your own horn
Collaboration	Collaboration/Competition	Bullying
Accepting Responsibility	Accepting Responsibility	Blame
Truth	Truth	Lies/Embellishments
Carbon Copies (transparence)	Carbon Copies (transparence)	Blind Copies (hidden copies)
Inclusion of the right people	Inclusion of the right people	Keeping key persons out of the loop
Paraphrasing and probing to test for understanding	Paraphrasing and probing to test for understanding	Unclear language/leaving out information
Controlling, directive	Participative	Controlling and manipulating
Open agenda	Sharing the right information at the right time	Hidden agenda
Substance	Taking responsibility, focus on substance and facts	Form (eg. Name dropping/status seeking)

Table 15.4: Differences between Political Styles.
Source: © 2011, Organizational Soul, Ltd.

Table 15.3 has two purposes. Firstly, it is designed to help you identify how you engage or detach from politics in the workplace. Secondly, it demonstrates how substance based and form focused behavior can manifest, so you can integrate these two types of behaviors to manage yourself, and the power dynamics of a situation optimally.

Communication and Political Behavior

Your ability to communicate effectively with integrity is central to a politically-competent strategy. Charismatic, persuasive, or influential people can manipulate a situation to achieve goals for the greater good or to accomplish their personal agenda. Politically-competent individuals are more interested in the team and can use the same persuasive skill set for team building and creating cohesion. Unconscious emotional patterns can drive under-political, overly-political, and savvy behaviors. Consequential thinking driven by your value system will determine your political-engagement strategy.

In an overly-political environment, many things may be left unsaid, so if you want to survive in this type of environment, you need to learn to read between the lines. In a predominantly under-political environment, the majority, who value substance over form, will say things to reflect those sentiments. Overly-political people can manipulate this information, because either they can predict others' thinking or others have told them what they think. Both of these situations can lead to low morale. The ideal is to consciously evolve into a politically-savvy person, harnessing the characteristics of the under- *and* overly-political types. Using the savvy style, you are equipped to survive any type of environment.

1 Rick Brandon and Marty Seldman, *Survival of the Savvy: High-Integrity Political Tactics for Career and Company Success.* (New York; Free Press, 2004).

2 Gary Zukav, *The Seat of the Soul,* (New York; Simon & Schuster, 1989), p. 26.

3 Gary Zukav and Linda Francis, *The Heart of the Soul: Emotional Awareness.* (New York; Free Press, 2001), p. 256.

4 Rick Brandon and Marty Seldman, *Survival of the Savvy: High-Integrity Political Tactics for Career and Company Success.* (New York; Free Press, 2004).

5 Rick Brandon and Marty Seldman, *Survival of the Savvy: High-Integrity Political Tactics for Career and Company Success.* (New York; Free Press, 2004).

6 Rick Brandon and Marty Seldman, *Survival of the Savvy: High-Integrity Political Tactics for Career and Company Success.* (New York; Free Press, 2004).

CHAPTER 16

DEVELOPING OTHERS

Make something of yourself. Try your best to get to the top, if that's where you want to go, but know that the more people you try to take with you, the faster you'll get there and the longer you'll stay there.

—James A. Autry

OVER the years, the best leaders with whom I have worked took time to mentor and coach me. They didn't do it from a place of forced obligation. Instead, they took the time to help me work on my strengths and some of my weaknesses, and it was their support, guidance, and ability to see a higher version of me that developed and stretched me.

I remember years ago when I was in college, a visiting professor in a lecture series said something I will never forget. He said it is not always the people at higher levels within an organization who pull you up to the top; it is more often the people who report to you who support you up through the organizational ranks. His presentation made a deep impression on me, and throughout my career, I spent time developing people, whether they reported to me or not.

What that visiting professor didn't say then—but I recognized later in my career—is that a byproduct of developing others is my personal and career development. One reason for this is that developing others freed my time up so that I could be exposed to strategic initiatives and new experiences early on in my career. A trained, engaged, creative team allows you to step out of the realm of doing and into a space of becoming.

Empower Yourself and Your Team

Members of your team can grow and develop if you create a safe space for them to operate. A safe space is an environment where different opinions and ideas are respected and cultivated. In a safe space, people need to be comfortable enough to be vulnerable and make mistakes. If fear creeps into the space, it is compromised.

Another way to create safe space to serve is to let go of your need to control people or situations and allow ideas that diverge from yours. If you are a leader, it is important to understand that encouraging different points of view can be constructive, so avoid letting your biases terminate or manipulate conversations. Instead, learn to cultivate people's ability to generate new ideas. This adds to the quality and diversity of information that goes into a collective solution.

When you are a leader attempting to create safe space, avoid letting your biases take root through constant complaining about members of your team. There are the usual complaints that team members are lazy, incompetent, or not giving 100 percent. Whatever the complaint, members of the team can sense the leader's true feelings. This can be disempowering because these employees are of the opinion they are not valued. The best leaders hold the members of their teams in the highest vision of themselves. They believe in their team and their ability to create synergies despite the prevailing weaknesses. They do not exaggerate the weaknesses of their team members; instead, they harness their strengths, and when a team member is not the right fit, they take action.

Tips for Developing Others

There are a number of ways that leaders can develop members of their teams. The following four suggestions are not always considered as developmental tools:

- Develop others through stretch projects
- Coaching
- Allowing
- Self-regulation

Develop Others through Stretch Projects

Create Stretch Projects

Stretch projects are an important mode of developing others. You can give employees a project to help them develop in areas where they demonstrate potential. Stretch projects take the learner beyond their comfort zone and can generate stress. As a coach or mentor, acknowledgment or recognition will help learners know that they are on the right path. When assigning a stretch project, effective feedback from the coach or mentor is integral to the development of the learner.

> **stretch project:** a project designed to push the envelope and develop a person's abilities.

Here are a few guidelines to help you to assign stretch projects:

Assign the right project to the right person

This is a basic guideline. The person to whom you delegate should have the right skill set or the potential to carry out the assignment with support. You can support the person or assign someone else the responsibility.

Know when the stretch is no longer a stretch

It is important for team leaders to develop the ability to determine when the stretch is no longer a stretch. This could happen if the assignment is too easy or when it becomes a burden or a destructive process. Stretch projects that go wrong can undermine the self-esteem of the person assigned the project, because sometimes the leader assigning the project miscalculates a person's will, strengths, or potential and assigns a project that overwhelms and paralyses the person.

Alternatively, the stretch may no longer be a stretch because the work is no longer a challenge. Learn to recognize this so that you can adapt your project assignments as your employee evolves.

Coaching Fundamentals

In a work environment, there are multiple opportunities to coach your peers or direct reports. There can be coaching for leadership and other behaviors, coaching for performance, even career coaching. Dr. Sally Jensen stated that "a coach is someone who will help you articulate your goals, define strategies and plans, hold a vision of you in full expression and success, and challenge you to achieve that vision."[1]

Author and trainer, Martin Sage, asserted that coaches use many different tools in the transformation process. Here are three of the tools he recommends as building blocks for coaching and developing others:

- Observation
- Making distinctions
- Feedback[2]

Observation

Observation entails being aware of yourself and others. It involves watching, filtering, and thinking critically. Coaches who are adept at observing are good at listening. They are capable of being still, tuning in, and discerning nuances.

Making Distinctions

Martin Sage said, "Having distinctions comes in and crashes your model of the world. In this realm, what we are trying to do is not figure out the truth, but we are trying to figure out what is truer than the model we've been operating on."[3] Making distinctions is about perceiving subtle differences when others can only recognize similarities. By making a distinction, you are articulating differentiating nuances in a way that creates clarity.

Making distinctions is especially useful when the person you are coaching can benefit from reframing a situation. For instance, by making distinctions you can coach people to separate their emotions from the decision-making process by helping them to separate fact from opinion. The primary goal is to bring clarity and balance.

Feedback

While listening, making distinctions, and observing are important components of the coaching communication model, so is providing feedback. Feedback provides coached employees with information that can help to identify opportunities to self-correct both internally through transformed thinking and externally through modified behaviors. It is important that the coach does not constantly criticize when giving feedback. Effective or constructive coaching feedback is developmental, which means at times it can be firm, lenient, and challenging. Constructive feedback acknowledges growth or progress and is designed to give the employee the courage to go beyond their level of comfort.

Effective feedback is supportive, appropriately timed and clearly articulated so that it can be understood by the receiver. A clue that you achieved an effective communication exchange is that at the end of a coaching or developmental conversation, the learner may have received honest information that was tough to digest yet feels clear, empowered, engaged, and committed to the next steps.

Allowing

Another way you can develop others is to give the learner the space to explore, be curious, and make mistakes. Impulses to control are not usually optimal, because learners who prefer to explore favor experimentation and are open to making mistakes if the environment is a safe one. Ara Parseghian, a former American football player and coach asserted that "a good coach will make his players see what they can become rather than what they are."[4] This requires allowing the person you are developing the latitude to attempt unconventional solutions and break tradition.

If you are not allowing latitude, the person you are mentoring is more concerned with getting everything right and executing directives the way you expect. If you are influencing someone to dissect situations from your perspective, you will end up creating a clone instead of helping the learner to accentuate his inherent talents. I recognize that it could be difficult to allow someone's unique style to emerge, because you have spent your whole life developing and becoming intimately acquainted with your own style.

Self-Regulation

Some people allow their unbridled emotions to get in the way of developing others. Impatience, frustration, jealousy, and insecurity are only some of the emotions that can impede your ability or motivation to develop others. For instance, there are long-tenured employees who are unwilling to train newcomers. These employees are usually concerned that the newcomers will overtake them in their careers.

Developing others requires emotional competence, because you may have to prepare yourself to let your vision go to prepare someone else to succeed you. Your vision may be something you nurtured during your entire career, but changing times and changing generations could mean one consequence of developing others is a makeover of your vision.

---

1 "What is Coaching?" on Dr. Sally Jensen's website, Dissertation Doctor, accessed, December 2009, http://www.dissertationdoctor.com/coaching/defined.html.
2 Martin Sage, "Coaching Skills" (Course, Sage Innovations, New York, NY, September 2005.)
3 *Ibid.*
4 "Ara Parseghian Quote of the Day", The Telios Group website, accessed December 2009, http://www.theteliosgroup.com/quotes/be-a-good-coach.

CHAPTER 17

EMOTIONALLY INTELLIGENT LEADERSHIP

People will rise to meet seemingly insurmountable obstacles and challenges if they understand the worthiness of the personal sacrifices and effort. Supporting that understanding must be mentors who provide leadership; without both ingredients, a cause will go unrealized and a mission is likely to fail.

—Glenn R. Jones

There is no singular, best leadership style, but an emotionally intelligent leader is capable of utilizing different styles depending on emotional and other dynamics behind the circumstances. Emotionally intelligent leaders who care about team building attempt to bring about transformation. Other types of leaders are more transactional, focused primarily on getting the work done and are out-of-touch with the needs of staff. Emotionally intelligent leadership (EIL) is essential to helping you navigate past your positive and negative biases and helping you to select a leadership style that best fits the circumstances.

Leadership Styles

Emotionally intelligent leadership (EIL) involves balancing relational and task-driven behaviors to improve and sustain leadership effectiveness. As a leader, emotional intelligence can help you understand whether a person will feel frustrated by or accepting of a leadership style, because you are able to appropriately respond to what they need from you. Emotional intelligence will cause you to refrain from micromanaging strong performers. It will also help you understand whether employees will be immobilized by fear and confusion if you give them an unstructured project with very little guidance.

Task-Centered Leadership Styles

A task-driven leadership style is focused on tasks and not relationships. Task-driven team leaders take an autocratic or coercive approach focusing purely on desired results. We often refer to this style as micromanagement because employees on the receiving end feel suffocated and controlled. This is because when a leader demonstrates a task-driven leadership style, power resides with the leader only. This style is appropriate when there is no time for discussion or if members of the team are not adequately trained to assume the responsibility delegated.

However, team leaders who apply this style with competent employees are perceived as unsupportive of the development of capable employees, because they treat skilled team members as though they are operating at low competence levels. When proficient team members are constantly confronted by a task-centered style, they can become frustrated and eventually lose interest in innovating, refusing to take action until they receive specific directives. Some competent employees eventually opt to leave the organization, because when a task-centered leadership style is inappropriately applied it can invoke emotions of anger, frustration, or hopelessness despite the employees' strong performance.

In an attempt to apply a task-centered style, some leaders become a source of delays and bottlenecks, because there is so much information to review, they are unable to deal with urgent matters and make decisions without causing missed deadlines and the appearance of incompetence for themselves and the persons waiting for decisions. This dynamic causes disrespect, frustration, or anger within persons reporting to the task-centered, unresponsive decision maker because of ill-timed feedback.

Pacesetting is about leading on the cutting edge; it is usually closely related to implementing innovation. According to Daniel Goleman, the pacesetting leadership style should be used sparingly, because it can negatively impact the organizational climate if implemented inappropriately[1]. If the team leader and employees are all competent, this style is low on guidance and can lead to high stress levels and exhaustion in both strong and weak employees because of the pressure.

While being a part of a pacesetting team can be a positive, exciting experience, the pacesetting leadership style can sometimes lean toward task-centeredness. This can occur if the leader takes a micromanaging approach because of competence deficiencies or high stress levels that lead to lowered productivity. Unfortunately, because some pacesetters are more focused on legacy, they may ignore the signs that their style is creating burn-out. When pacesetters lose sight of the people side of change, they contribute to a toxic task-centered environment.

While task-centered styles can be the result of promoting persons naturally predisposed to demonstrating controlling behavior, sometimes the behavior is the result of an organizational culture that does not tolerate mistakes or risk taking. For instance, if a leader is told there is no room for error or if they inherited a skill-deficient team, fear may drive their controlling behavior. If fear is a motivator, some task-centered leaders may hold onto work that can be delegated in order to ensure a consistent, controlled standard of output.

Relationship-Centered Leadership Styles

One type of relationship-focused leadership style is a collaborative style. It is based in trust and designed to sustain constructive, consistent participation that can lead to individual and collective transformation. From a perspective of power distribution, when collaboration occurs, power and risks are shared by employees and leaders, because employees are invited to share their ideas and opinions. If leaders are not overly-analytical, a collaborative approach can lead to an integrative, optimized solution.

From an emotionally-competent perspective, a relationship-focused, collaborative leadership style can help team members feel valued by the organization and when the style is applied appropriately, it can lead to the development of employees and the building of overall employee morale. Relationship building skills, such as appreciation, consistency, listening, and asking questions to engender self-reliance all contribute to confidence and competence building.

The collaborative style can be used as a developmental style for high performers. This happens when employees are provided with stretch goals designed to take them beyond their internally-perceived barriers in preparation for building self and organizational trust in their competence, ethics, and consistence. By creating opportunities for assuming additional responsibility, emotionally intelligent leaders create the possibility for significantly reducing the need for guidance.

Despite the fact that a leader may focus on relationship building, commitment levels of employees on the team can vary. Reasons for varying levels of commitment can range from an employee not being interested in the job because of impaired recruitment practices to indiscernible, negative cultural dynamics within the team. Latent, negative cultural dynamics can result from peer pressure to underperform and maintain the status-quo.

A non-interfering style can be a relationship-dependent leadership style where a manager delegates full control of the process and outcome. In this context, the non-interfering style is based in trust, and the trust level is much higher than in the collaborative style because required guidance is minimal. It involves full relinquishment of power by the leader because the employee has proven competence and a consistent track-record, so decision-making authorities are delegated even though an inappropriate decision can negatively impact the performance of the leader.

Choosing a Leadership Style

When deliberating an optimal leadership style, combination of styles, or sequence of styles to apply to your circumstances there are a number of considerations you can use to integrate into your decision:

1. Identify the Stakeholders
2. Consider Your Options
3. Time Your Approach

Identify the Stakeholders

When choosing a style or style mix you will need to first identify the stakeholders in the decision or the people you will affect by your decision. Stakeholders include, but are not limited to, your direct reports, your reporting manager, executives, members of the board, and your clients. Once you identify the stakeholders with a primary interest in your decision, determine which relationships are important to the decision in the short to long term. You also need to understand the relevant power structures within the organization and how relational considerations will impact your results.

Consider Your Options

When considering your options, first understand your problem, keeping in mind the possibility that a short-term positive solution can lead to long-term, negative repercussions. Remember also to consider your assumptions, and criteria for making your decision before contemplating alternative outcomes.

It is important to take a step back and think about your options instead of allowing the circumstances to trigger a thoughtless response. As a leader you can react to situations or you can respond. Reactions are actions driven by emotions that override thought, logic and fairness. A response is thoughtful, using critical and consequential analysis to avoid a purely emotional reaction.

Time Your Approach

Once you identify your stakeholders and how you want to manage your relationships with them, your timing needs to be precise. Timing needs to be considered from the perspective of when you should time your leadership intervention(s), and once you decide when you will begin, you will need to determine how long you will sustain your approach before considering course correction or termination.

Emotionally Intelligent Leadership (EIL) Competencies

While we have already explored the following emotional intelligence competencies, the list below summarizes the competencies needed if you choose a relationship building leadership style:

1. Self-awareness
2. Self-regulation
3. Optimism
4. Effective communication
5. Balancing people and task considerations
6. Embracing conflict

7. Connectivity (empathy)
8. Fairness

Self-Awareness

Self-awareness helps you to become aware of your patterns of emotion and behavior, and once you hone this skill, you are equipped to use it to diagnose fluctuations in morale that may occur because of latent or existing conflict before it escalates to an intractable position.

Self-Regulation

This skill is critical in the context of leadership, because as a leader, your negative moods or responses can create emotional contagion, triggering negative emotions in others, and if sustained, contagion can lead to low morale. Self-regulation is especially necessary when communicating with coworkers. Self-regulatory behavior requires examining the consequences of your actions and making a conscious decision to respond so that fairness and level-headedness prevail.

Self-regulation in the context of EIL is also connected to demonstrating consistent behavior. Your actions should be consistently fair and measured, considering the policies and integrating human factors. The inability to understand the consequences of your decisions will directly undermine your ability to lead effectively.

Finally, regulating yourself by sustaining consistency is about aligning your statements with your actions. Leaders who do not maintain the integrity of their words and actions will not be trusted or respected.

Optimism

There are some leaders who feel disempowered by limited resources, controlling executives, or constant change. Optimistic leaders are capable of focusing more on the strengths of members of the team and setting the stage for those employees to develop in the area(s) of their talent or potential. These leaders are not unrealistic in their optimism; they recognize that they could be wrong about the employee's latent capacity, because the employee may not have the capability, confidence or will to respond favorably to developmental overtures. Optimistic leaders are able to sustain their commitment to development of others, and they are also able to detach and treat the employee respectfully, fairly, and empathetically if there are performance obstacles that cannot be overcome.

Effective Communication

When leaders are disrespectful in their communication patterns, employees will typically view this as abusive. If disrespectful communication is sustained employees are not motivated to achieve their full potential within their environment, because they are forced to switch from self-actualization mode to survival mode. When leaders are listening actively and behaving respectfully and authentically, they can build trust and collaboration, because employees usually want to feel that their contributions count.

Communication is dynamic, occurring at various levels. It is both verbal and non-verbal, so there is always room for misinterpretation because of emotional and other listening barriers. Emotionally intelligent leaders manage their emotions, exhibiting discipline about distinguishing between factual- and opinion-driven information. Leaders who effectively communicate, understand that when they impart knowledge they should ensure the information is understood and there is buy-in before appropriate action can ensue. They understand the veracity of body language and filter this information, responding constructively, building and sustaining safe space. They also realize there can be obvious and hidden meanings, so they seek clarification, avoiding assumptions based on biases.

Balancing people and task objectives

Emotionally intelligent leaders are capable of balancing relational and task objectives in a way that they can be effective in their roles. As previously stated, they recognize that sometimes a transactional approach to leadership is necessary, and they know when it is appropriate to exhibit this style. They also know which relationships are important and how to maintain those relationships so that objectives such as team building can be achieved.

Embracing Conflict

Whether trust is present or not, true leaders embrace conflict. At its core, conflict indicates there are competing ideas or purposes. While some leaders fear conflict and avoid it at all costs because of personal security needs, others are driven by the need to build the team, so they engage conflict using developed self-regulation and advanced communication and influence skills.

True leaders embrace conflict whether it is latent or not. They demonstrate courage and respect during the process while balancing various points of view and synthesizing this information into a solution. Emotionally intelligent leaders are unafraid of making difficult decisions, and they know what to do to manage relationships when unpopular decisions are unavoidable.

Connectivity and Empathy

Emotionally intelligent leaders are capable of perceiving unproductive patterns of behavior and seeking information that will expose root emotional and other causes. When considering emotion in the workplace, the only way an emotionally intelligent leader can connect to people's needs at a root level is with adequate trust between the leader and staff. If trust is absent or deficient, employees will be reluctant to admit, expose, or explore deeper issues. Some will even act as though the perceived unproductive behavior is a figment of the leader's imagination.

The ability to empathize is an ability to demonstrate compassion without being viewed as a pushover. It requires insight to know when a softer approach is appropriate or when a tougher approach will be more compassionate or empathetic.

Fairness

Fairness implies the capacity to view multiple perspectives, and remain true to the objective of team building when making the decision. It requires the ability to set aside your personal biases and make decisions that may sometimes be viewed as unpopular.

When fairness is present, appropriate transparence can also occur. Demonstrating fairness in an environment where there is no trust will still create mutations in perception that will result in a general feeling of partiality.

In this type of environment, transparence is not possible until the level of trust is improved.

Fairness also includes the ability of the emotionally intelligent leader to ensure that accountability exists equitably among members of the team. Emotionally intelligent leaders accept responsibility when the team does not perform as well as expected. They avoid blame and excuses, admitting culpability and demonstrating integrity.

Competence, Commitment, and Engagement

There is the underlying expectation that leaders possess a sound understanding of the competence and commitment levels of their team members, so they are aware of how decisions will impact team morale. Emotionally intelligent team leaders are able to detect whether an employee is competent, committed, or engaged by monitoring the employee's behavioral patterns. Competence is indicative of both the existing technical and behavioral skill levels of the employee. Commitment is driven by buy-in, confidence, trust, or interest levels. When commitment is low, this is usually interpreted as an attitudinal or behavioral challenge. Commitment is not the same as engagement. Some employees commit to doing a good job because of their work ethic, but they are not engaged, connected members of the team, so they exhibit detached behavior when team interaction is necessary. They engage the work but not their coworkers.

The list below explores different combinations of competence and commitment in an effort to provide insight into how these components directly impact morale or engagement.

High Competence, High Commitment

This employee possesses strong technical skills and is comfortable with her ability to perform. She may be more skilled than her team leader, and if the team leader's self esteem is intact, this can lead to opportunities for free reign and stretch projects. Generally, this employee is highly engaged and intrinsically motivated. She has high confidence levels and is an asset to the organization if she is aligned with the vision of the organization.

High Competence, Variable Commitment

The highly-competent person with variable commitment is experienced and capable, but may lack the confidence to fly solo, or the will to be consistent. It is important to understand the reason behind the variable commitment. If the variation is related to low trust levels, trust-building activities can be implemented. If variable commitment levels are related to disagreement with instructions, skills such as listening and persuasion can be used by the leader to understand the root causes. If the team member is a high performer and easily influenced by negative team members, an attempt can be made to counterbalance the negative influencers with positive feedback.

High Competence, Low Commitment

The highly-competent employee with low commitment is competent, but she is not very committed to her work. She may occupy a role that is too easy, a role that is of no interest to her, or she may be in a highly dysfunctional work environment with impaired trust levels. As a leader, you will have to ascertain the cause of the low commitment in order to determine which leadership style you should use, because low commitment levels can lead to deficient results.

It is conceivable that despite low commitment levels, this type of employee may apply herself and attain results because of a strong work ethic. A strong work ethic can give the appearance of high commitment, so instead of low productivity, the low commitment level can manifest in the form of a resignation letter or a request for a transfer.

Some Competence, High Commitment

The employee with some competence and high commitment may or may not have the ability to improve his performance. As a leader, it is up to you to determine whether there is potential for performance improvement and whether a supporting leadership style can develop him. This type of person already has a high level of commitment, so if he is in the wrong role and can offer value to the company, he can be considered for redeployment to an appropriate role. Otherwise, there is the risk that his commitment may diminish. Another example of a person with some competence and high commitment is when an employee is highly committed and possesses the required technical competencies, but his interpersonal skills are deficient. This reduces the impact of the technical skill on the team, because it can lead to dysfunctional interactions.

Some Competence, Variable Commitment

This employee may or may not possess the ability to improve her performance. When an employee has some competence and variable commitment, leaders need to determine the root cause(s) of the underdeveloped competencies and variable commitment because competence levels may have an effect on commitment levels or vice versa. For instance, when an employee is promoted beyond her capacity to perform satisfactorily, a variable commitment dynamic can emerge.

This competence/commitment combination can occur both with new employees and longer-tenured employees. For instance, long-tenured employees may possess some competence because of years of repetition, but they lack an understanding of why they do what they do. Variable commitment can exist in cases such as this because the employee has not developed beyond a transactional role after multiple years of service.

Some Competence, Low Commitment

The employee with some competence and low commitment possesses some of the necessary competencies/skills but is unable to perform satisfactorily without strong direction or constant follow up. This can happen if the role or situation is new, or if the employee was placed in a role that exceeds his capabilities. A task-centered leadership style can be implemented depending on the causes for low commitment and competency gaps. Alternatively, options for the employee's best fit can be contemplated.

Low Competence, High Commitment

This person does not possess the basic skills necessary to perform competently, but he is highly committed to the job and the team. As a leader, you will have to assess whether he possesses the potential to be trained or whether he can be placed in another role. When commitment is high, decision makers sometimes delay a decision to offer a separation package. This can happen when loyalty is important or if the employee adds value in another way. For instance, the employee may be a confidant for their coworkers and can help to mitigate retention or other people risks. Unfortunately, employees with low competence and high commitment do not always positively influence their coworkers by demonstrating high commitment levels if their colleagues are burdened with additional work.

Low Competence, Variable Commitment

This employee does not possess the basic skills needed for the role she occupies but she is somewhat committed to the job/team or organization. The employee's commitment level may be variable because she is new to the team or because of the dynamics created by the quality of work relationships. Another reason for her variable commitment level may be because she doesn't perceive many career opportunities outside the organization so she feels forced to stay because she needs the job.

If the employee's competence levels can be improved through developmental opportunities, her commitment levels may improve because her confidence will grow. If the person was promoted beyond her capacity or if she is not interested in the job, it will be very difficult for her to evolve to higher competence or commitment level.

Low Competence, Low Commitment

This person lacks the specific skills required for his role, and as a result, his confidence and motivation levels are low. If developmental opportunities will not lead to improved competence or commitment levels, separation or alternative placement should be contemplated. If the team member possesses the potential to develop the desired competencies, but he does not possess the will to develop himself for a particular role, the selling style can be used so that development can occur.

If the person possesses the potential but shows no interest in improving his performance, your efforts to set the stage for performance building will be fruitless. In cases like this, members of the team may have developed hardened negative attitudes that may be reinforced by underperforming, influential co-workers.

Morale Attunement

Morale represents the collective mood or emotion of a team. As an emotionally intelligent leader, it is important for you to be attuned to morale, understanding how to see past surface behaviors and into the authentic dynamics. For instance, if trust is absent in a department, employees may convert to survival mode and appear to be happy with the organization. Some leaders read this literally, not understanding the context of the behavior, and therefore they overlook the deeper needs of employees.

Morale is a moving target that can be influenced by both external and internal factors. The first step in developing awareness is for a manager is to obtain a true diagnosis of morale through an employee opinion survey, focus group sessions, or individual interviews. Keep in mind that if, as the team leader, you are one of the sources of low morale and you plan to interview your team about morale, employees will not be entirely open with you about all the root causes.

Once you diagnose the root issues, the next step is to manage your emotions. Refrain from going into defense mode, blaming, or becoming emotional about opinions of employees. It is more important to be fair and balanced in dealing with the issues uncovered so you can avoid turning the action-planning process into a witch-hunt designed to ascertain the source of qualitative and quantitative survey information.

Building morale requires building relationships, and if trust in leadership is impaired, a trust-building exercise ought to be part of the morale building process. In addition to the competencies previously articulated in this chapter, morale-building activities include:

1. Challenging long held, negative beliefs, helping employees to reframe their thinking into a more constructive framework.
2. Treating individual issues individually and team issues collectively. This means you should not address individual issues collectively. Targeted employees rarely take responsibility for their actions when issues are presented to the team, because chances are that your target audience is blissfully unaware that they are being targeted, as their behaviors have not been addressed individually.
3. Action planning and execution of the plan are critical once you

diagnose the root concerns. When planning, be sure to involve trusted, competent change champions to assist you with shifting the morale. These change agents should be respected by both you and the team population.

4. Recognizing the part you play in perpetuating low morale and publicly commit to changing your behavior; then change your approach.

5. Providing employees with opportunities to develop or advance to the next level on their career paths.

6. Appropriately recognizing employees for their contributions to the team. Insincere rewards are easily perceived.

When a culture is characterized by complacency and entitlement, no matter what leaders do, employees feel they are being short-changed. Sometimes this is because of unhealed, past altercations or unpopular decisions. Other times it happens because leaders do not manage performance effectively. When that happens, employees may have an inflated sense of their contributions and feel underappreciated. In some circumstances, this type of culture is perpetuated by the negative modeling of managers and executives who complain about the organization and demonstrate apathy and entitlement.

Emotionally intelligent leaders take the time to understand whether and how they are influencing complacency or entitlement. They then self-regulate, because they recognize they cannot influence new behaviors if they are still demonstrating the old, limiting patterns. Sometimes managers and executives are immobilized when it comes to addressing their negative behaviors. They are unable to change their own behaviors, because they want to be accepted by others, and the change will inevitably cause alienation.

Emotionally Intelligent Leadership (EIL)

Emotionally intelligent leaders can be catalysts for transformation and healing, because they are attuned to the needs of employees and can pre-empt obstacles to daily performance and interactions. Emotionally intelligent leaders:

- Adapt to Context
- Are Effective Change Agents

- Value Others

Adaption to Context

Emotionally intelligent leaders are able to observe circumstances from a macro level, modify their behaviors based on the unique needs the situation, and communicate using an appropriate style. At a deeper level, emotionally intelligent leaders understand the attitudes, strengths, and limitations of the team, so they manage everyone's expectations, keeping them balanced and realistic.

We previously examined an example in which a team leader assigned a person to a role, and the person was not performing. The decision created an uneven distribution of work, because the leader had to rely on the more competent workers to complete their work and the work of others. The stronger performers started to feel they were being unfairly used. An emotionally intelligent leader would typically coach the non-performing employee, and if there were no change after providing the employee with opportunities to improve, the leader would not hesitate to assist with the transfer or termination of the employee, recognizing inaction as a grave disservice to the team. The emotionally intelligent leader would recognize that the redistribution of the non-performing employee's work would only serve to negatively impact the morale of the team.

Effective Change Agents

In any change circumstance, at least two components of change require attention: the human element and the process. Typically, changes to the process need to be scoped, redesigned or replaced, and implemented, so your team can move to completion.

Some team leaders neglect the people component of change until the implementation phase, when members of the team are more prone to resist the change initiative, because they were not consulted earlier to attain buy-in. In cases like this, the communication strategy ends up being a rushed afterthought that is predictably deficient. There are several reasons why leaders can be ineffective in midst of change. For instance, leaders may miscalculate the effect of emotional contagion related to job insecurity issues such as job loss,

loss of status, or the uncertainty regarding their ability to grasp the change and operate at a competent level within a reasonable amount of time.

Emotionally intelligent leaders are able to understand the consequences of neglecting to involve the right people in the scoping and planning stages of the change initiative. They also understand the human dynamics of change and create a flexible communication plan that addresses the fears of the team, seeks to provide clarity, is adequately timed, and consciously maintains top-down and bottom-up channels of communication.

Emotionally intelligent leaders manage team morale during the change process by harnessing the enthusiasm of early adopters while simultaneously keeping the resistors in balanced perspective. As already established, resistors can create barriers because of fear, but anger and frustration can also contribute to their refusal to accept the change.

In a changing environment, policies need to be written or rewritten, procedures developed, and training designed in order to effectively assuage fears of employees. As a leader, you can ensure training or retraining is provided to everyone who will experience changes in their roles. This will help to eliminate or reduce the fear of the unknown and anxiety related to low levels of competence. Effective, emotionally intelligent leaders are able to recognize and gracefully manage the complex human aspects of change, ensuring the right balance exists between process and human considerations.

Valuing Others

Emotionally intelligent leaders are able to demonstrate that they value members of the team. This is because they are able to demonstrate this quality and engender similar behaviors within other team members by highlighting and rewarding desired behaviors. However, based on experience, there are reasons why engaged employees leave despite the existence of strong leadership. One reason is that they can decide to leave because their values or life circumstances change.

Some team leaders support a healthy, competitive work environment in theory but may not possess the skills necessary to ensure that competition remains healthy. In cases like these, competition can become dysfunctional if the team leader is not conscious about human dynamics and skilled enough to manage undermining interpersonal behavior.

For instance, when team leaders espouse team building as a value but only reward competitive, high performers, unhealthy dynamics infiltrate the team. In such cases, the value for individual high performance supplants the value for team performance because of a lack of leadership skill, fear of diminished results in the short term, a lack of experience with detecting inconsistent behavior, or a lack of integrity.

If a team leader regularly assures employees that he values members of the team, but his decisions are based on personal goals such as obtaining a promotion or being accepted, the personal agenda can corrupt the decision-making process and lead to defective results.

Another behavior that demonstrates the leader does not value others is the action of having all the answers. As previously stated, know-it-alls cause employees to feel voiceless, and this dynamic can lead to employee detachment and low morale. In those cases, when know-it-alls attempt to demonstrate that they value others, employees usually perceive their actions as shallow or inauthentic, and they will tend to reject the leader's overtures.

Emotions and Leadership

EIL is an integral part of achieving individual and collective E.Q. Librium, because diversity, constant change, and external demands can all lead to frustration. When leaders apply the same style to everyone on the team, frustration will inevitably surface, because each individual has different needs for direction from leaders.

The emotionally intelligent leader demonstrates emotional and other intelligences. They are capable of authenticity, capacity building, knowing how much effort to exert, when it is appropriate to withdraw, how to apply pressure when needed, and when to provide opportunities for growth.

---

1. Daniel Goleman, *"Primal Leadership: learning to Lead with Emotional Intelligence,"* (Boston Massachusetts, Harvard Business School Press, 2004) p 72–75

CHAPTER 18

EMOTIONAL INTELLIGENCE AND DIVERSITY

I have found that an environment that is welcoming and highly inclusive creates increased levels of trust, which in turn results in higher levels of productivity and better outcomes.

—Thomas L. Sager

Diversity refers to your ability to embrace differences in others. Because your thoughts and emotions are directly connected, diversity involves the ability to understand, your emotions and manage your responses.

Cherobosque, Gardenswartz and Rowe of the Emotional Intelligence and Diversity Institute made the following statement about diversity and emotional intelligence: "EID (Emotional Intelligence and Diversity) involves the ability to feel, understand, articulate, manage and apply the power of emotions to interactions across lines of difference."[1] The dimensions of diversity we encounter in the workplace include: Age, appearance, cognitive skill, emotional competence, race, gender, status, economic background, religion, sexual orientation, communication skill, and education.

Diversity and Bias

We tend to gravitate toward persons who are similar to us and we experience varying levels of discomfort with persons who differ. When we are aware of ourselves and are interacting respectfully, opportunities for constructive, inclusive, authentic responses occur regularly. When we are unaware of ourselves, we may unintentionally respond negatively to familiar and unfamiliar circumstances. The following list outlines possible unregulated, negative reactions to any type of stimulant based on your biases and negative assumptions:

Intolerant, Biased Responses:

- Attack the circumstances or the speaker
- Reject the situation
- Defend your position
- Conquer the situation
- Interfere with the plan (through passive aggression or overt sabotage)
- Avoid the issue
- Hesitate because you don't trust or understand the circumstances
- Fear, anger, jealousy, impatience and other emotions

As we have already established, your biases are powerful influences on your emotions and behaviors. Therefore, it is important to learn how to circumvent or reframe your underlying beliefs so you can destabilize unproductive biases.

In a diverse work environment, it is optimal for you to respect other people's beliefs and choices. According to Tulin Diversi Team Associates, a coaching, consulting, and training organization, you have three choices when responding to a situation that requires a diversity conscious, considerate approach:

1. You can maintain your beliefs and behaviors.
2. You can maintain your beliefs and modify your behaviors.
3. You can challenge your beliefs and allow new paradigms to form while breaking old ones. In a diverse environment, this sets the stage for the formation of new, inclusive behaviors.[2]

Culture and Emotional Intelligence

Cherbosque, Gardenswartz, and Rowe created an EID competence called intercultural literacy. They state that it, "involves understanding each others' cultural rules, norms, and values, and being able to empathize and metaphorically walk in their shoes. It also encompasses resisting the temptation to judge others' behavior by our own standards by seeing the advantages and disadvantages of all cultural norms."[3]

To develop your intercultural literacy, your value systems can remain intact, but an understanding of why people do what they do can lead to patience, and inclusive behaviors. Cherbosque, Gardenswartz, and Rowe also asserted, "This awareness and knowledge (of intercultural literacy) helps us to 'read' the behavior of others more accurately so we can deal with them more effectively."[4]

> **intercultural literacy**: the ability to demonstrate sensitivity toward various cultural traditions without compromising the significance of one's own cultural identity.

In the same way you can develop your emotional literacy by building your emotional vocabulary, you can develop your cultural literacy by taking the time to gain an appreciation of different backgrounds, traditions, points of view, and family norms. So it is important to take the time to understand your coworkers, because learning about why differences exist can help you understand their behaviors, motives, drive, and value systems.

People are generally tight-lipped about their private motives and value systems so it will take time to build trust and openness. You can contribute to improving trust levels by demonstrating curiosity as opposed to judgment. Keep in mind that trust building is a reciprocal process, so it will behoove you to take risks and share information strategically. Seeking to understand another person's cultural background is important, because it brings clarity into the equation. Clarity will help you to avoid making irrelevant, unfair, or inaccurate assumptions based on past programming.

Tolerance vs. Inclusion

Tolerance

Tolerance means different things to different people. For the purpose of this exploration, tolerance is about putting up with a person or a situation. This suggests your underlying bias is a deeply-embedded value system, and while your actions may typify actions without prejudice, the person on the receiving end of the communication experiences discomfort because of perceived judgment emanating from you. Tolerance can be perceived as disingenuous or fake, as it is difficult to connect with others when you perceive them as bad or wrong because they are different. Despite your best efforts, your bias tends to seep through during the interaction.

Tolerance can also refer to agreeing to disagree. In a situation such as this, you can make your case known (your disagreement), but you will put up with the other person or group of persons, because you know you are unable to convert their thinking and you need to get along. Again, this approach is judgment based and does not facilitate connection.

Tolerance can generate emotion because your coworkers sense they are not being accepted by you. Their ability to perceive helps them to sense your toxic emotions of fear, impatience, and superiority.

Inclusion

On the other end of the spectrum is the ability to connect through inclusive behaviors. Some people can empathize and connect, because they naturally embrace differences. While they may have a different view, it is not important for them to impose their views on anyone else. There are others who demonstrate inclusive behaviors who may learn something new by interacting with persons who are different. Based on the new knowledge acquired through interaction, they may decide to change their beliefs about a group of people. In a case like this, transformed thinking can lead to constructive interactions.

Integrating inclusive behavior across the organization is one of the primary objectives of developing diversity conscious behaviors whether you are a leader or not. Demonstrating inclusive behavior can help build teams, encourage creativity and innovation, facilitate the needs of clients and program an organization for future success. Inclusion can also improve internal HR processes like recruitment, succession planning, talent management, and overall decision making. The following tips are designed to help you to transition closer to diversity conscious behavior:

- Perceive differences as opportunities to strengthen solutions by integrating different views when possible.
- Avoid only focusing on differences; attempt to see the similarities between you and the people on your team.
- Avoid labeling *different* as *wrong*.

- Recognize your own biases and prejudices.
- Develop a level of comfort with ambiguity and exhibit flexibility.
- Avoid allowing anyone else's biases to affect your point of view. Alternatively, avoid adopting or projecting your positive and negative biases.
- Learn to use optimism to view people and their differences as potential assets, not as opportunities for frustration.
- Listen to other viewpoints without feeling threatened. Then integrate these perspectives into a solution where possible.
- Respect differences without feeling or exerting pressure to change.
- Write and speak using respectful, inclusive, and sensitive language. Refrain from using words such as "you people," "they," and "them." Instead, use inclusive language, such as "us" and "we."
- Learn conflict resolution strategies and how to mine for conflict. This will help you proactively circumvent bullying and unnecessary eruptions of anger, fear, or frustration.
- Create an atmosphere of inclusion by modeling inclusive behavior.
- Create safe space for open dialogue and listening. One way to achieve this is to reward inclusive behaviors. Another way to achieve this is to avoid divisive statements and nonverbal actions.
- Avoid accusatory, blaming language.
- Author Martin Sage describes a skill that works in the context of diversity: learning how to tie in the other person's argument so they will listen[5].

An underlying assumption that comes through the list of inclusive behaviors is that in order to achieve diversity awareness and acceptance, it would be optimal if you could manage the individual and collective belief systems that lead to division and master communication skills that build cohesion. No matter your position in an organization, your ultimate goal is to communicate from a place of authenticity, develop others, and build your skill of mining for conflict before it erupts into an intractable state of coexistence.

1 Jorge Cherbosque, Lee Gardenswartz, and Anita Rowe. *Emotional Intelligence and Diversity*, (Mountain View, CA; CCP Inc.), p 1

2 Tulin DiversiTeam Associates, *Business Excellence Through Diversity Seminar* (Wyncote, PA, 2003)

3 Jorge Cherbosque, Lee Gardenswartz, and Anita Rowe. *Emotional Intelligence for Managing Results in a Diverse World*, (Mountain View, CA; CCP Inc., 2008).

4 Ibid

5 Martin Sage, "Coaching Skills" (Course, Sage Innovations, New York, N.Y. 2005)

CHAPTER 19

THE IMPORTANCE OF EMOTIONAL INTELLIGENCE TO THE ORGANIZATION OF THE FUTURE

We are all moving into the workplace of the future together. It is all about competing for the best people. And the best people are thinking about their work lives in a whole new way. [Employers] have to lose their attachment to the old-fashioned career path. We can all learn from the emerging workforce and generation.

—Bruce Tulgan

EXPERTS predict numerous changes in the next fifteen years, so this chapter explores some of the predicted changes that will affect how we interrelate and why emotional intelligence will become an increasingly indispensible bundle of skills.

Hyper-Change Is in the Forecast

We always hear the cliché "change is the only thing that is constant," and this has yet to be disproven, because no matter how dramatic or incremental, shift happens. In our current context, many people are finding that change is not only constant, but it is also frequent and intense.

In their 2008 report, "Trends Shaping Tomorrow's World," Marvin

Cetron and Owen Davies state that "an individual's professional knowledge is becoming outdated at a much faster rate than ever before ... Rapid changes in the job market and work-related technologies will necessitate job education for almost every worker. At any given moment, a substantial portion of the labor force will be in job retraining programs."[1] Therefore, if organizations don't get better at managing hyper-change, they will be stuck in reactive mode facing compounding challenges.

From an emotional competence perspective, hyper-change translates into higher levels of pressure and stress. When resources are less available and higher levels of stress are constant, there is more potential for conflict and organizational politics if leaders are not conscious about attaining E.Q. Librium.

Desynchronization

Desynchronization is another source of hyper-change. It occurs when one organization or industry evolves at a much faster rate than its suppliers or other external agencies. Because of desynchronization, the faster developing agency will face frustration, because their pace of change is unmatched by collaborating agencies. Consequently, the slower-paced agencies will be frustrated by demands to create efficiencies that may represent undesired expenses.

The Wirearchical Model

Jon Husband, change researcher and consultant, predicts that we will move from a predominantly static hierarchical model of organizing companies to a combined hierarchical and "wirearchical" model. This new model is defined by Jon Husband as, "an informal but pervasive emerging structure of governance, strategy, decision making, and control based on knowledge, trust, meaning, and credibility. Things get done and results are achieved through the interplay of vision, values, connections, and conversation. Wirearchy is generated by an open architecture of information, knowledge, and focus, enabled by connected and converging technologies."[2]

With the potential of wirearchy, there could be an enhancement in dynamics within organizations that can be facilitated by the application of emotional intelligence tools. Jon Husband does not predict that a wirearchy will replace the hierarchical model, but it will transform it. In the wirearchical system, the emphasis will no longer be placed as heavily on organizational charts as organizational flow. Under the new system, the spotlight will be on facilitating the flow of power, information, connections, and conversations.

Transparent Organizations

Internal and external organizational stakeholders are demanding more transparency and the dissolution of borders. According to the 2010 *Harvard Business Review* article, "Leadership in the Age of Transparency" by Christopher Meyer and Julia Kirby, in an age of transparency, there is growing accountability. There is no room for arrogant companies that take advantage of loopholes or ignore their impact on communities, because stakeholders are holding companies more and more accountable. Meyer and Kirby stated, "Given the heightened sensibilities of ordinary people, any apparent callousness by corporations is more likely to raise hackles."[3]

External pressures can create internal demands within corporations that sometimes require an immediate, well thought-out response. Emotional intelligence will play a very important part of any leader's tool kit given the emerging complexities of doing business in a modern, changing environment. External pressures create the need for a response, responses create the need for responsible change, and change can lead to uncertainty or progress, depending on the context of the change.

Multigenerational Coexistence

According to a 2005 Deloitte publication, *Who are the Millennials, AKA Generation Y,*[4] "Millennials" are people who were born roughly between 1978 and 1995—as opposed to Generation X, born between 1961 and 1977—and they are the largest generation after the baby boomers.

Millennials are characterized as follows:

- They are multitaskers and very open to challenges.
- They are open to change.
- They are computer, cell phone, and electronically literate.
- They enjoy networking.
- They are easily bored. They seek to enjoy their work and are more prone to leave their job faster than any of the other generations if they are not happy.

- They are entrepreneurial.

As Millennials continue to infiltrate the workforce, Baby Boomers are still present because they are retiring later and later. Baby Boomers are very different; they are sometimes defined as a workaholic generation placing high importance on career achievement and face-to-face communication. They thrive in competitive environments and relish their independence. With three different generations with very different value systems coexisting in the workplace, there is sustained need for emotional competencies in all age groups.

In a January 2008 article, author Steff Gelston stated, "Relations among the generations seem to be at a low point. Generation Y (defined as people born after 1982) thinks Generation X (spawned between 1961 and 1981) is a bunch of whiners. Generation X sees Generation Y as arrogant and entitled. And everyone thinks the Baby Boomers (1943 to 1960) are self-absorbed workaholics."[5]

So as more and more Generation Ys enter the workplace and move up the hierarchy, emotional intelligence will be central to the optimal balance and flow of communication, power, authority, turnover, and employee morale. Baby Boomers value a strong work ethic and feel that Generation Ys are slackers who need to work harder. Generation X and Baby Boomers believe in face-to- face or phone conversations. Generation Y prefers texting, blogs, or social networks as communication platforms. This creates a communication gap, because Generation Y is not at their best in face-to-face communication or conflict.

As the generational changes influence how we do business, the highly controlling constructs established by Baby Boomers will be replaced by more fluid flow structures. As more virtual teams emerge, the texting Generation Y may be a good fit for the evolution. However, there will be a period where the incompatibilities will continue to create contention, and this is where emotional intelligence and diversity-awareness skills are needed.

New Skills for the Future

In addition to multigenerationalism, Tessa Finlev predicts that new competencies will be needed to survive in the workplace of the future. Some of them are reliant on emotional intelligence skills. For instance, Finlev describes a skill called *Emergensight* which is "the ability to prepare for and handle surprising results and complexity that come with coordination, cooperation, and collaboration on extreme scales."[6] Navigating your emotions, consequential thinking and empathy, and optimism are all underlying emotional intelligence skills that serve as building blocks for Emergensight.

Another skill Finlev foresees is Signal/Noise Management, which involves "filtering meaningful information, patterns, and commonalities from the massively-multiple streams of data and advice." Building the skills of pattern recognition and consequential thinking are fundamental to developing the skill of signal/noise management. Both skills require the distillation of meaningful information in situations that range from simple to complex. These skills are especially useful in constantly changing environments where there is high potential for uncertainty and fear.

One last skill in Finlev's list of ten workplace skills for the future is what she calls Cooperation Radar. This is the "the ability to sense, almost intuitively, who would make the best collaborators on a particular task or mission."[7] The emotional intelligence skills of consequential thinking, navigating your emotions, empathy, and optimism can form the foundation for developing this skill. In some cases, a person's skill level will be clear, but in some circumstances, noise management will be necessary to attempt to predict a person's capacity to collaborate effectively. No longer will strong technical competencies be the primary deciding factor. The right behaviors will now have an increasingly heavy weight.

In a dynamic era, emotional intelligence is now an imperative. It is a fundamental building block that is the foundation for achievement of both individual and organizational E.Q. Librium. Ideally, emotional self-mastery will give you the edge you need to not only survive increasingly complex environments but to lead a balanced and successful life.

1 Cetron, Marvin and Owen Davies, "Trends Shaping Tomorrow's World." Report published by the World Future Society, May–June 2008.
2 "Do Knowledge Workers and Knowledge Managers Face Much More Change?" on John Husbands' a website Wirearchy, accessed September 2009, http://www.wirearchy.com/impo rted-20100202172716/2009/6/16/do-knowledge-workers-and-knowledge-managers-face-much-more-c.html.
3 Chris Meyer and Julia Kirby, "Leadership in the Age of Transparency," in *Harvard Business Review, April 2010*.
4 Deloitte Development LLC, "Who are the Millenials, AKA Generation Y?" (2005).
5 Steff Gelston, "Gen X, Gen Y, and the Baby Boomers: Workplace Generation Wars," posted on the CIO website, January 30, 2008, accessed December 2009, http://www.cio.com/

article/178050/Gen_Y_Gen_X_and_the_Baby_Boomers_Workplace_Generation_
Wars?page=1&taxonomyId=3185.

6 "10 Workplace skills of the Future; The Skills Workers Should Strive to Have and the Skills
Employers Should Seek Out and Promote," by Tessa Finley on the Institute for the Future
website, May 8, 2009, accessed December 2009, http://www.iftf.org/node/2774.

7 *Ibid.*

GLOSSARY

THE definitions listed in the Glossary are from the following sources: Merriam-Webster; linguaspectrum.com; wordnetweb.princeton.edu; wiktionary.org; Wikipedia; generalhealthtopics.com; focusaimachieve.com; relationshipmanagementinstitute.com; poeticbyway.com; Critical Thinking Handbook.

action plan: a focused, disciplined, and thoughtful approach to achieving goals. This includes career and personal goals.

active listening: an engaged listening mode that allows the listener to understand and evaluate what is being said. The skills of paraphrasing information from another party and using probing questions to gain a better understanding are typically used to clarify the meaning of what is being said.

authentic power: power that is derived from an internal source of integrity. People who demonstrate authentic power take full responsibility for their experiences or emotions. Authentic power is connective, because it is based in internal congruence and empathy. The demonstration of authentic power can lead to others demonstrating their own authentic power.

awareness: the state of possessing or having a realization; a demonstration of perception of a person or concept.

blame: a self-preservation tactic based on fear. The antithesis of integrity and being held accountable for ones actions.

cognition: mental processes. The rational activities of the mind. The part of mental function that deals with logic, as opposed to affective, (i.e. emotional).

commitment: an agreement (verbal or written) or pledge to perform some action in the future.

conflict resolution: the ability to resolve conflicts between disagreeing parties in an effective manner.

consequential analysis: the ability to identify and understand the consequences or alternative results of one's actions.

critical thinking: exercising or involving careful judgment in evaluating a situation.

disclosure: the act of making a previously hidden revelation evident.

emotional competence: the essential social skills needed to recognize, interpret, and respond constructively to emotions in yourself and others.

emotional intelligence: a form of social intelligence that involves the ability of monitoring your feelings and emotions and those of other people, discriminating among them, and using this information to guide your thinking and actions.

emotional virus: the transference of emotional responses from one party to another.

emotion: a conscious mental reaction that is subjectively experienced and typically accompanied by a physiological response.

empathy: the ability to experience the emotions of another party. The feeling or capacity for awareness, understanding, and sensitivity one experiences when witnessing, hearing or reading of some event or activity of others, thus imagining the same sensations as that of those actually experiencing them.

envy: the desire to possess the same advantage that one witnesses in another individual or party.

E.Q. Librium: the ability to identify personal emotions and the emotions of others and filter that information into a balanced, holistic, and self-regulated response.

feelings: Sensation, particularly through the skin; emotion; impression; emotional state or well-being; emotional attraction or desire; intuition; an opinion, an attitude; emotionally sensitive.

force: the use of tactics designed to give a person an advantage over an individual or group. It is coercive: to cause to do through pressure or necessity, by physical, moral, or intellectual means.

gossip: idle talk or rumor, especially about the personal or private affairs of others. It forms one of the oldest and most common means of sharing (unproven) facts and views, but also has a reputation for the introduction of errors and other variations into the information transmitted; a person engaging in such activites.

honesty: fairness, truth, and straightforwardness in conduct with others. Not disposed to cheat or defraud; not deceptive or fraudulent.

influence: the power to affect, control or manipulate something or someone; the ability to change the development of fluctuating things such as conduct, thoughts or decisions; an action exerted by a person or thing with power over another.

intercultural literacy: the ability to demonstrate sensitivity toward various cultural traditions without compromising the significance of one's own cultural identity.

jealousy: an emotion that typically refers to the negative thoughts and feelings of insecurity, fear, and anxiety over the anticipated loss of either something that a person values or a perceived advantage.

life coach: a professional individual who guides people to their greatest potential by overcoming obstacles and making commitments that demonstrate measured progress. A life coach works one-on-one with a client to support personal growth, behavior modification, and goal-setting.

morale: a state of individual psychological well-being based upon a sense of confidence, usefulness, and purpose; the mental and emotional disposition of a group with regard to tasks and functions of group operation.

office politics: the use of one's individual or assigned power within an employing organization for the purpose of obtaining advantages beyond one's legitimate authority. Those advantages may include access to tangible assets, or intangible benefits such as status or pseudo-authority that influences the behavior of others.

organizational culture: a codified system of behaviors and mannerisms that is taught to a group and transferred to new members. It is the set of beliefs, values, and norms, together with symbols such as events and personalities that represent the unique character of an organization and provide the context for action in it and by it.

pessimism: a state of mind in which one perceives life in terms of negativity, expecting the worst.

resilience: is the positive capacity of people to cope with stress and catastrophe. It also includes the ability to bounce back to homeostasis after a disruption.

self-confidence: self-assuredness in and self-awareness of one's personal judgment, ability, and power.

self-discipline: correction or regulation of oneself for the purpose of personal improvement. Having the ability to control one's desires and impulses.

situational ethics: a Christian ethical theory that was principally developed in the 1960s by the Episcopal priest Joseph Fletcher. It states that sometimes moral principles can be cast aside if love is best served.

stress: a physical, chemical, or emotional factor that creates a difficulty that causes worry, bodily, or emotional tension.

stretch project: a project designed to push the envelope and develop a person's abilities.

value systems: a set of consistent personal and cultural standards used to determine ethical integrity.

yielding: a willingness to comply or submit to the requests of another. One can yield in a battle in order to win a war, so yielding does not have to imply giving up the vision.

BIBLIOGRAPHY

Aron, Elaine N. *The Highly Sensitive Person: How to Thrive When the World Overwhlems You.* (Portland, OR; Broadway, 1997).

Barsade, Sigal. "Managing Emotions in the Workplace: Do Positive and Negative Emotions Drive Performance?" *Academy of Management Perspectives.*

Benjamin, Bill. "Emotional Intelligence Training: Case Study—Medrad." *www.selfgrowth.com.*

Bennet, Bo. *Year To Success.* (Massachusetts; Archieboy Holdings LLC, 2004)

Berne, Eric. *Transactional Analysis in Psychotherapy,* (New York; Ballantine Books, 1986.)

Branden, Nathaniel. *The Power of Self Esteem: An Inspiring Look at Our Most Important Psychological Resource,* (Florida; Health Communications Inc. 1992)

Burris, Ethan. "Missing Voices," Jan. 2010, *www.utexas.edu.*

Cetron, Marvin and Owen Davies, "Trends Shaping Tomorrow's World." *The World Future Society,* 2008.

Cherbosque, Jorge, Lee Gardenswartz, and Anita Rowe. Emotional Intelligence and Diversity, (Mountain View, CA; CCP Inc.) p.1.

Emotional Intelligence for Managing Results in a Diverse World (Mountain View, CA; CCP Inc., 2008).

Covey, Steven. *The Seven Habits of Highly Effective People.* (New York; Free Press, 2004).

Crandall, Susan. *Thinking About Tomorrow: Reinventing Yourself at Midlife.* (New York; Grand Central Publishing, 2009).

Deeter-Schmelz, Dawn R. and Jane Z. Sojka, (1993). "Developing Effective Salespeople: Exploring the link between emotional intelligence and sales performance," International Journal of Organizational Analysis, Vol. 11 Iss: 3, pp. 211–20

Deloitte Development LLC. (2005). "Who are the Millenials?—a.k.a. Generation Y."

Dobbs, Kevin. "Knowing How to Keep Your Best and Brightest." *Workforce,* April 2001.

Dreamer, Oriah Mountain, *The Invitation,* (New York; Harper Collins, 2006.)

Dyer, Wayne W. *You'll See It When You Believe It: The Way to Your Personal Transformation,* (New York; Harper, 2001).

Elder, Linda. "Cognition and Affect: Critical Thinking and Emotional Intelligence." *Inquiry: Critical Thinking Across the Disciplines,* Winter, 1996. Vol. XVI, No. 2.

Facione, Peter A. *Critical Thinking: A Statement of Expert Consensus for Purposed of Educational Assessment and Instruction.* (Millbrae, CA; California Academic Press, 1990).

Finley, Tessa. "10 Workplace Skills of the Future: The Skills Workers Should Seek Out and Promote." *www.iftf.org.*

Fletcher, Joseph. *Situation Ethics.* (Calgary, AB; Canadian Institute for Law, Theology, and Public Policy, 1999).

Freedman, Joshua. "Assessing Trust." *www.6seconds.org.*

Gelston, Steff. "Gen X, Gen Y, and the Baby Boomers: Workplace Generation Wars." *www.cio.com.au.*

Goleman, Daniel. *Emotional Intelligence: Why It Can Matter More Than IQ.* (New York: Bantam, 1997).

Green, Robert. *The 48 Laws of Power.* (New York; Penguin, 2000). Gurd, Vrendi. (2007). "Mind and Body: The Physiology of Our Emotions." *www.trusted.md.com.*

Heart2Heart. "Self-Empowerment: The Wow Factor." *www.heart-2-* heart.ca.

Hsieh, Diana Mertz. "What is Objectivity?" *www.enlightnement.supersaturated. com.*

Husband, John. "From Hierarchy to Wirearchy: The Future of Workplace Dynamics." *www.wfs.org.*

Jensen, Dr. Sally. "What is Coaching?" *www.dissertationdoctor.com.*

Jordan, Peter J. (2004). "Emotional intelligence in teams: Development and initial validation of the Short Version of the Workgroup Emotional Intelligence Profile (WEIP-S)." *Journal of Management & Organization. www.e-* contentmanagement.com.

Kerr, Robert et al. (2006)."Emotional Intelligence and Leadership Effectiveness." Leadership & Organization Development Journal, Vol. 27 Iss: 4, pp. 265–79.

Kilmann, Ralph and Kenneth W. Thomas. *Thomas-Kilmann Conflict Mode Instrument.* (Mountain View, CA; CCP Inc., 1974).

Last, Walter. "The World of Feelings and Emotions." *www.health-* science-spirit.com.

Lencioni, Patrick. *The Five Dysfunctions of a Team: A Leadership Fable.* (Hoboken, NJ: Jossey-Bass, 2002).

Lipton, Bruce H. *Biology of Belief: Unleashing the Power of Consciousness, Matter, and Miracles.* (Carlsbad, CA; Hay House, 2005).

Lowenstein, Dr. Tim. "Life Stress Test," *www,stresmarket.com.*

Luskin, Dr. Frederick. *Forgive for Good: A Proven Prescription for Health and Happiness,* (New York; HarperOne, 2001)

Mann, Fredrick. "How to Achieve and Increase Personal Power."

(West Hollywood, CA; 1993). Retrieved from *www.buildfreedom.com*.

Menon, Tanya and Leigh Thompson. "Envy at Work." Harvard Business Review, April 2010. *www.hbr.org*.

Meyer, Chris and Julia Kirby. "Leadership in the Age of Transparency." Harvard Business Review, April 2010. *www.hbr.org*.

Mind Tools Ltd. "Root Cause Analysis: Tracing a Problem to Its Origins." *www.mindtools.com*.

Mwangi, Innocent. "Breaking Free from Self Limiting Habits." *www.ssmk.net*.

National Association of Church Personnel Administrators. "Characteristics of Healthy Working Relationships." *HR Connect*, vol. 1, Issue 30, April 2005.

Parseghian, Ara. "Quote of the Day." *www.theteliosgroup.com*.

Perera, Karl. "Self Esteem if the Key to Your Happiness and Well Being." *www. more-selfesteem.com*.

Pert, Candace Ph.D, *Molecules of Emotion*. (New York; Simon and Schuster, 1999).

Peters, Tom. "The Brand Called You." Fast Company (1997)

Prism Ltd. "What is Commitment?" retrieved at *www.prismltd.com*.

Rampersad, Hubert. *Effective Personal and Company Brand Management: A New Blueprint for Powerful and Authentic Personal and Company Branding*. (Charlotte, NC; Information Age Publishing Inc., 2008).

Reily, Anne and Tony Karounos, "Expolring the Link Between Emotional Intelligence and Cross-Cultural Leadership Effectiveness." *Journal of International Business and Cultural Studies*.

Salovey, P. and J. D. Mayer. (1990). Emotional intelligence. *Imagination, Cognition, and Personality*, 9, 185–211.

Sasson, Remez. "Will Power and Self-Discipline."*www. successconsciousness. com*.

Satchidananda, Sri S. *The Yoga Sutras of Patanjali: Commentary on the Raja Yoga Sutras.* (Buckingham, VA; Integral Yoga Publications, 1990).

Schawbel, Dan. *Me 2.0: Build a Powerful Brand to Achieve Career Success,* (New York; Kaplan 2009).

Schein, Edgar. (2001). "Organizational Culture and Leadership." *Classics of Organization Theory.* Jay Shafritz and J. Steven Ott, eds. 2001. (Fort Worth: Harcourt College Publishers).

Seligman, Martin E. P. *Learned Optimism: How to Change Your Mind and Your Life.* (New York: Knopf, 1991).

Shoshanna, Dr. Brenda. "Four Steps to Becoming Closer (Developing Emotional Intimacy), *www.selfgrowth.com.*

Sklare, John. "Change Your Thinking, Change Your Life." *www.lifescript.com*

Sobel, Andrew and Jagdish Sheth. *Clients for Life: How Great Professionals Develop Breakthrough Relationships.* (New York; Simon & Schuster, 2000).

Spencer, L. M., Jr. et al. *Competency Assessment Methods: History and State of the Art.* (Boston: Hay/McBer, 1997).

Techxellent Traning Solutions. "Anthropomorphic Robots: Could Robots Ever Duplicate Humans?" *www.techxellenttraining.com.au.*

The Mayo Clinic. "Forgiveness: Letting Go of Grudges and Bitterness."*www. mayoclinic.com.*

Thorndike, E. L. (1920). "Intelligence and its uses." *Harper's Magazine* 140: 227–35.

Tuckman, Bruce, Dennis Abry, and Dennis R. Smith. *Learning and Motivation Strategies: Your Guide to Success.* (Upper Saddle River, NJ; Prentice Hall, 2001).

Tzu, Lao, *Tao Te Ching,* (600 B.C.E.)

Velasquez, Manuel, Claire Andre, Thomas Shanks, and Michael J. Meyer.

"Thinking Ethically: A Framework for Moral DecisionMaking."www.scu. edu.

Wilde, Oscar. Lady Windermere's Fan. Act III (1892 Play)

Wright, Judy H. "Setting Boundaries in Relationships." *www. artichokepress. com.*

Zenzen, Thomas G. "Achievement Motivation." unpublished paper. (Stout, WI; 2002).

Zukav, Gary and Linda Francis. *The Heart of the Soul: Emotional Awareness.* (New York; Free Press, 2001).

Zukav, Gary. *The Seat of the Soul.* (New York; Simon & Schuster, 1989).

WORKS CONSULTED

Berlo, David K. *The Process of Communication.* (New York: Holt, Reinhart, and Wilson, 1960).

Blanchard, Kenneth H., Paul Hersey, and Dewey Johnson. *Management of Organizational Behavior* (Upper Saddle River, NJ; Prentice Hall, 2001).

Brandon, Rick and Marty Seldman. *Survival of the Savvy: High-Integrity Political Tactics for Career and Company Success.* (New York; Free Press, 2004).

Fletcher, Joseph. *Situational Ethics.* (Calgary, AB; Canadian Institute for Theology, Law, and Public Policy, 1999).

Greenbaum, Michael, (2000). "Emotional Intelligence Takes Customer Loyalty to a Higher Level," *Business and Management Practices, Boardwatch Magazine,* Vol. XIV, No. 7; Pg. 120–2.

Maslow, Abraham. "A Theory of Human Motivation." A.H. Maslow (1943) Originally Published in *Psychological Review,* 50, (1943) 370-396.

Riemer, Marc J. (2003). "Incorporating Emotional Intelligence (EQ) Skills into the Engineering Curriculum to Facilitate Communication Competencies." *World Transactions on Engineering and Technology Education,* Vol. 2, No. 2.

Sage, Martin, "Coaching Skills" Course, *Sage Innovations,* New York 2005.

Sage, Martin, "Time and Money," *www.globalcoachingnetwork.net/ courses/index.htm.*

Six Seconds Emotional Intelligence website and blog, *http://www.6seconds.org*

INDEX

48 Laws of Power, The, 120, 132, 219

A
Abry, Dennis A., 79
Accommodating Style, 148
Achievement Motivation, 79, 222
Action Plan, Creating An, 92
Allowing, 74, 87, 103, 107, 126, 139, 178, 181, 187, 205
Anger, 21, 23, 56, 60-61, 67-68, 70, 83, 94, 99, 101, 104, 109, 121, 134-135, 137-138, 151, 165, 168, 184, 198, 202, 205
Aron, Elaine, 70-71, 217
Authentic Power, 168-170, 213
Avoiding Style, 148

B
Baby Boomers, 209-212, 218
Barriers to Listening, 138
Barsade, Sigal, 67, 71, 217
Behavioral Patterns, 15, 63, 159, 191
Benjamin, Bill, 49, 56, 217
Bennett, Bo, 136, 142
Berlo, David K., 29, 223
Berne, Eric, 143, 166, 217
Bias, 26, 44, 103, 115, 141, 154, 201, 203-204
Big-Picture Perspective, 161, 163-164
Biology of Belief, 128, 219
Blame, 51, 101, 117, 121-125, 141, 191, 213

Blame Free Environment, 124
Blind Spot, 76, 78, 108
Boyle, Emily, 42, 47
Branden, Nathaniel, 111, 116, 217
Brandon, Rick, 167, 176, 223
Bullies, Costs of, 159
Bullying, 16, 120, 157-160, 205
Burris, Ethan, 128, 132, 217

C
Certon, Marvin, 207, 208
Cherbosque, Jorge, 206, 217
Coaching Fundamentals, 180
Cognition, 29, 82-83, 88, 213, 218, 220
Collaborative style, 146, 185-186
Commitment, 74, 79, 89, 101, 122, 186, 189, 191-194, 214, 220
Communication, 8-9, 28-29, 32, 36, 50-55, 65, 68, 71, 77, 99, 103-104, 118-120, 127-128, 130, 133-141, 144, 146, 152-156, 158, 162, 166, 176, 181, 187, 189-190, 197-198, 201, 203, 205, 210, 223
Communication Loop, 118, 137-138, 155
Communication Skills, 50, 138-139, 153-154, 190, 205
Competence, 15, 26-29, 33, 38, 65, 71, 80, 96, 110, 125, 127, 140-141, 144, 150-151, 156, 163, 166, 170, 173-174, 182, 184-186, 191-194, 198, 201-202, 208, 214

Competing Style, 146, 173

Complainer, 140, 152

Complaining, 151, 178

Compromise, 78, 125, 138, 147, 149, 156, 173-174

Conflict, 17, 29, 53, 62, 98, 127, 143-151, 153-157, 160-166, 172, 187-188, 190, 205, 208, 210, 214, 219

Conflict-Driven Environments, 149

Conflict Resolution, 143-146, 148-149, 151, 154, 156, 162, 166, 172, 205, 214

Consquential Analysis, 77

Courage, 42, 73-74, 93-94, 99-100, 102, 122, 181, 190

Covey, Steven, 71, 217

Crandell, Susan, 95-96

Critical Feedback, Model, 152

Critical Thinking, 82

Critics, Types of, 153

Curiosity, 28, 32, 53, 80, 133, 141, 151, 154, 156, 203

D

Davies, Owen, 208, 211, 217

Deeter-Schmelz, Dawn R., 50, 57, 218

Desynchronization, 208

Developing Effective Salespeople, 50, 57, 218

Developing Others, Tips for, 178

Differences between Political Styles, 175

Difficult People, Types of, 150

Disclosure See also Honesty, 140

Diversity, 17, 121, 153, 172, 178, 199, 201-202, 204-206, 217

Drama Attractor, 150, 155

Dyer, Wayne, 161, 166, 218

E

Effective Personal and Company Brand, 95, 220

EIL, 183, 187-188, 196, 199

Emergensight, 210-211

Emotional Intelligence, 13, 15-17, 21-22, 27-29, 31-32, 34, 36-39, 41-44, 46-47, 49-53, 56-57, 61, 65, 73, 76, 79-81, 88-89, 96-98, 101, 104, 110, 120, 124, 128, 133-134, 136-137, 143-145, 148, 150-151, 153-154, 156, 165, 170, 172-174, 183, 187, 199, 201-202, 206-211, 214, 217-220, 223

Emotional Intelligence and Diversity (EID), 201

Emotional Intelligence and Leadership, 42, 46-47, 219-220

Emotional Intelligence and Leadership Effectiveness, 42, 47, 219

Emotional Intelligence in Teams, 43, 47, 219

Emotional Reaction, 23, 84, 187

Emotional Virus. See Viral Transmission, 67, 76

Emotional Vocabulary, 23, 60-61, 203

Emotionally Competent Communication, 133

Emotionally Intelligent Leadership, 183, 187, 196

Emotions, 15-17, 21-24, 26-29, 31-32, 35-39, 41-44, 46, 50, 52, 54, 56, 59-62, 65-67, 69-71, 73-77, 79-83, 85-88, 91, 93, 96, 99, 101-102, 104, 107-109, 113, 115, 117, 121-122, 124, 126, 128, 135-138, 140-141, 145, 147, 150-151, 154, 161, 164-166, 168, 174, 180, 182, 184, 187-189, 195, 199, 201-202, 204, 211, 213-214, 217, 219

Empowerment, 120, 136

Engagement, 130, 191
Engaging Others, 161, 164
Envy, 117, 119, 121, 132, 214, 220
Envy at Work, 119, 132, 220
E.Q. Librium (Emotional Intelligence Quotient), 16, 27-29, 31, 34, 47, 87, 105, 154, 199, 208, 210-211, 214
Exploring the Link between Emotional Intelligence and Cross-Cultural Leadership Effectiveness, 46-47

F
Facione, Peter A., 82, 88, 218
Fairness, 28, 104, 141, 156, 187-188, 190-191, 215
Financial Management, 32, 38
Finlev, Tessa, 210
Five Dysfunctions of a Team, 54, 57, 219
Fletcher, Joseph, 100, 104, 216, 218, 223
Flexible optimism, 75
Force, 47, 73, 82, 136, 143, 146, 168, 170-171, 208, 215
Forgiveness, 28, 99, 102-104, 163, 221
Freedman, Joshua "Assessing Trust", 51, 218
Frustration, 21, 33, 56, 91, 99, 109, 134, 155, 162, 165, 182, 184, 198-199, 205, 208
Fundamentalism, 157
Future, 34, 59, 74, 91, 96, 103, 115, 132, 147, 149, 173, 204, 207, 210-212, 214, 217-219

G
Games People Play, 15-16, 167, 170
Gandhi, Mahatma, 93, 129
Garvin, John, 42, 47
Gelston, Steff, 210-211, 218

Generation X, 209-210
Generation Y, 209-211, 218
Glad Game, The, 67
Goals, 32-35, 38, 59, 73, 79, 92, 95-96, 98, 102, 107, 111, 113, 121-122, 124, 153, 163, 176, 180, 185, 199, 213
Goldstein, Kurt, 136
Goleman, Daniel, 16, 41, 65, 81, 88-89, 184, 199, 218
Gossip, 55-56, 108, 173, 215
Green, Robert, 120, 132, 219
Gurd, Vreni, 65, 71

H
Halo or Horn Exercise, 85
Harvard Business Review, 119, 132, 209, 211, 220
Heaton, Norma, 42, 47
Hierarchy of Needs, 109, 111, 113, 133-134, 158
Highly Sensitive Person, The, 70-71, 217
Honesty, 140
Hostile, 126, 150-151, 157
Hsieh, Diana Mertz, 87-88, 219
Hurt, 23-24, 39, 75
Husband, Jon, 208
Hyper-Change, 207-208

I
Identify Your Biases, 83, 85
Identify Your Emotions, 27, 56, 60-61, 67, 121, 124
Inclusion, 203-205
Influence, 27, 41-42, 50, 80, 102, 122, 125, 129, 133, 190, 194, 196, 210, 215
Integrity, 28, 39, 42, 53-55, 67, 99-101, 123-125, 156, 167-168, 170-171, 174, 176, 188, 191, 199, 213, 216
Intercultural Literacy, 202-203, 215

Intrinsic Motivation, 33-34, 42, 46, 79, 113, 136, 151, 160, 163

J
Jealousy, 70, 117-121, 152-153, 182, 202, 215
Jordan, Peter, 43, 47, 219

K
Karounos, Tony, 46-47, 220
Kerr, Robert, 42, 47, 219
Kirby, Julia, 209, 211, 220

L
Last, Walter, 21, 29, 219
Leadership in the Age of Transparency, 209, 211, 220
Learned Optimism: How to Change Your Mind and Your Life, 37, 39, 80, 221
Learning and Motivation Strategies: Your Guide to Success, 79-80, 221
Lencioni, Patrick, 54, 57, 219
Lennick, David, 28
Liar, 156
Lights On, Lights Off Exercise, 89-91
Limiting Patterns, 107-108, 111, 196
Lipton, Bruce, 128, 219
Listening, 36, 84, 127-128, 137-140, 150-151, 161, 165, 180-181, 185, 189, 192, 205, 213
Love, 21-22, 32, 75, 80, 91-92, 100, 129, 135, 216
Luskin, 163, 166, 219
Luskin, Fredric, 163, 166, 219
M
Making Distinctions, 180-181
Managing Your Thoughts, 160-161
Maslow, Abraham, 79, 109, 134, 136, 142, 223
Mayer, John, 21

Me 2.0: Building a Powerful Brand to Achieve Career Success, 95
Medrad Study, The, 49
Menon, Tanya, 119, 132, 220
Meyer, Christopher, 209
Missing Voices, 128, 132, 217
Mission, 96, 112-113, 119, 183, 211
Morale Attunement, 195
Motivation, 33-34, 42, 45-46, 79-80, 90, 107, 109, 113, 116, 134, 136, 142, 151, 153, 160, 163, 182, 194, 221-223
Mountain Dreamer, Oriah, 74, 80, 218
Multigenerational Coexistence, 209
Multiple Points of View, 83, 86, 157
Mwangi, Innocent, 110, 116, 220

N
Nonverbal Communication, 77, 137, 139-140

O
Objectivity, 28, 83, 87-88, 102, 115, 219
Office Politics, 28, 167-168, 215
Optimism, 27, 37, 39, 46, 51, 53, 56, 60, 67, 74-75, 80, 93, 136-137, 151-152, 160, 162, 187-188, 205, 211, 221
Organizational Awareness, 41, 44
Organizational Culture, 44-45, 47, 128, 132, 185, 216, 221
Ownership, 99, 101, 122

P
Paradigm Shift, 113
Parseghian, Ara, 181-182, 220
Personal Brand, 95-96, 220
Personal Financial Management, 38
Personal Goals, 33-34, 107, 153, 199, 213
Personal Success, 31, 34, 95

Pert, Candice, 71
Pessimism, 51, 131, 216
Peters, Tom, 95-96, 220
Political, 15, 44, 99, 108, 110, 128-129, 131, 135, 147, 149-150, 155-156, 163, 167, 170-171, 173-176, 223
Political, overly, 15, 149, 156, 167, 170, 173-174
Political savvy, 110, 167, 170, 173, 176, 223
Political styles, 167, 174-175
Position Based Power, 171
Power, Authentic, 168-170, 213
Power Tactics, 168-169
Process of Communication, 29, 137, 223
Protectionist Mode, 129
Purpose, 32-35, 46-47, 51, 61, 69, 79, 89-96, 108, 111-113, 136, 168, 203, 215-216

Q
Quiet Desperation, 117, 130

R
Rampersad, Hubert, 95-96, 220
Recognize Your Patterns, 62, 65
Reframing, 51, 75-76, 113-115, 138, 180
Reframing Model, The, 113, 115
Relationship Building, 39, 185-187
Relationship Centered Leadership, 185
Reilly, Anne, 46-47
Resilience, 74-75, 216
Resourcefulness, 99, 104
Responsiveness, 99, 104
Rowe, Anita, 206, 217

S
Sage, Martin, 13, 180, 182, 205-206, 223

Salovey, Peter, 21, 29
Sarcasm, 24
Schawbel, Dan, 95-96, 221
Schein, Edgar, 44, 47, 128, 130, 132, 221
Sensitivity and Emotion, 70
Seldman, Marty, 167, 176, 223
Self-Actualization, 110, 112-113, 136, 189
Self-Awareness, 45, 65-66, 71, 77, 134, 187-188, 216
Self-Confidence, 41, 45, 50, 216
Self-Discipline, 43, 61, 73-74, 107, 133, 216, 220
Self-Esteem, 111-113, 120, 135-136, 148, 152-153, 163, 179
Self-Knowledge, 160-161
Self-Protectionism, 117, 128-129
Self-Regulation, 16, 46, 54, 73, 81, 93, 141, 144, 154, 160, 162, 178, 182, 187-188, 190
Seligman, Martin, 37, 39, 51, 75, 80, 221
Setting Boundaries, 53-54, 78, 222
Seven Habits of Highly Effective People, 71, 217
Situational Ethics, 99-100, 216, 223
Sklare, John H., 113, 116
Smith, Dennis R., 79-80, 221
Sobel, Andrew, 165-166, 221
Sojka, Jane Z., 50, 57, 218
Spencer Jr., L. M., 41, 47, 221
Strategic Implementation, 146-149
Stress Management, 38
Stressed-Out People, 150, 154
Stretch Projects, 178-179, 191
Substance focused people, 170
Survival of the Savvy, 167, 176, 223

T
Task Centered Leadership, 184

Team Leadership, 41, 43, 53, 127, 130, 149, 185, 219
The Glad Game, 67
The Highly Sensitive Person, 70-71, 217
The Process of Communication, 29, 223
The World of Feelings and Emotions, 21, 29, 219
Thomas-Kilmann Model of Conflict Resolution, 144-145
Thompson, Leigh, 119, 132, 220
Thorndike, E. L., 31, 39, 221
Tolerance, 111, 203-204
Transactional Analysis in Psychotherapy, 144, 166, 217
Transparent Organizations, 209
Tuckman, Bruce, 79-80, 221

U
Under-Political People, 170, 173-174
Understanding Your Power, 79
Unresponsive People, 150, 155

V
Value System, 28, 87, 97-98, 162, 170-171, 176, 203
Valuing Others, 198
Viral Transmission, 67, 76
Vision, 78, 93, 95-96, 112, 178, 180, 182, 191, 208, 216
Voicelessness, 117, 125, 135, 151

W
Wirearchy, 208, 211, 219

Y
Yielding, 78, 164, 216

Z
Zukav, Gary, 170, 176, 222

CPSIA information can be obtained at www.ICGtesting.com
Printed in the USA
BVOW04s2147240816

460096BV00017B/118/P